Ex Libris

☆

The cover
i l l u s t r a t i o n,
painted by W. P.
Greuling, is from
a photograph of a rare
scene in Boston Harbor,
February 12, 1941. Reminiscent
of the days a century ago when
the sailing ship was supreme, it shows
the four-masted bark *Abraham Rydberg,*
Swedish training ship, on arrival 69 days out
of Santos, Brazil. The photograph, by Andy Smith
for the Boston Transcript, is particularly
appropriate for use with this publication as
it contains the three prime elements of
pilotage — (a) the *Rydberg* desiring a
pilot, (b) the *Pilot* #1 which provided the pilot, (c) the "yawl,"
rowed by two apprentice boatmen, taking the pilot,
Captain George Poor,
to board the wait-
ing square-
r i g g e r.

☆

Pilots and Pilot Boats
of
Boston Harbor

Presenting
stories and illustrations
of the skilled, resourceful men of stout hearts who,
with their trim, weatherly boats of sturdy construction,
have played such an important role
in the maritime life of
Boston

By

RALPH M. EASTMAN

Privately printed for the

SECOND BANK-STATE STREET TRUST COMPANY
BOSTON, MASSACHUSETTS
1956

THE RAND PRESS

Boston

FOREWORD

In the following letter written some years ago by the late Charles H. Taylor, son of the founder of the Boston "Globe," to the late Allan Forbes, at that time President of the State Street Trust Company, the seed was planted which is now bearing fruit in this brochure.

"I am making a few notes on the suggested book on Boston Pilots while I still have the matter in mind.

"The idea is to have a history of pilotage in Boston with stories and pictures of early and also famous pilot boats and little sketches of some of the more famous pilots themselves.

". . . Besides this, in the old days the Boston merchants and others used to take their yachting trips with the pilots and go off for two or three weeks at a time. Capt. Dolliver entertained Daniel Webster, James Russell Lowell, Professor Agassiz, Henry Wadsworth Longfellow and many other notable men on the pilot boats. James Russell Lowell in his letters speaks of one trip which he made in the old pilot boat 'Friend' with Capt. Dolliver. Webster used to make the chowder which usually consisted of as much Madeira as chowder.

"Take it all in all, I am sure you can make a most interesting booklet and on a subject which has not been touched upon except in one or two newspaper stories. . . . Probably not one person out of a thousand who goes aboard and sees the pilot coming aboard or leaving knows that the pilots run their own game and finance themselves so I think you can strike an absolutely new and most interesting field."

We found early in our work that what he had said about the lack of published information was only too true but we hope that the following pages will be considered a worthy contribution to the printed material on the subject. Whether we have made "a most interesting booklet" is left for our readers to decide. However, we have tried hard to live up to Mr. Taylor's inspiring words. His cheerful assistance and constructive suggestions years ago were extremely helpful in enabling us to get on the trail of much of the information presented herein. Through him we also enjoyed the hearty cooperation of the late Charles M. Wright of the "Globe" staff who introduced us to the pilots and provided several photographs of pilot boats and many bits of pilot lore which were very useful.

It was a pleasure and a privilege to get to know the pilots, ranging in age from 24 to 58, all of whom seem to share the characteristics of physical fitness, competence and calmness which instinctively inspire confidence in the ability of the individuals to carry on their responsible duties thoroughly and ably.

* * *

This is the first of our brochures which has not had the benefit of the guidance and wisdom of Allan Forbes in its preparation. Naturally, a thread of sadness has run through the hours spent in research and compiling the material presented. Over the years, because of his sense of humor and kindly disposition, the time spent with him in going over manuscript and printer's proofs developed into a sort of game with each one trying to find something to be changed or corrected which the other had missed. His witty comments and sage suggestions, frequently mixed with amusing reminiscences, injected many bright spots in the work involved. This writer's sentiments are well expressed in the following lines by Lord Byron:

> Farewell! if ever fondest prayer
> For other's weal avail'd on high
> Mine will not all be lost in air
> But waft thy name beyond the sky.

* * *

When work on this volume was initiated one of the first recommendations on the part of the Boston pilots was that a visit of at least 24 hours on a pilot boat in the harbor was the best way to absorb the right atmosphere for writing about their activities. This trip is described briefly later in this volume.

A rather disheartening bit of news at the outset was that in a fire during the night of August 29, 1925 all of the early records of the pilots had been lost, thus eliminating a most promising source for research. However, we discovered a few (very few) of the newspaper stories mentioned in Mr. Taylor's letter. We wish to express our thanks to the "Globe," "Herald," and "Post," all of Boston, for their courtesy in granting us permission to use material from these articles. We also found an interesting article in the late Boston "Transcript" which proved helpful in our search for information on the events pertaining to pilotage half a century or so ago.

In taking up the study of pilotage service, one of the first things that is confusing to the novice is to find that the number on a pilot boat cannot be relied upon alone for identification. As boats went out of service their numbers were assigned to their replacements, so knowledge of the dates of operation is necessary in order to avoid complications in referring to them. Another point that requires explanation to the reader is that the rowboat used in transferring pilots to and from larger vessels is not actually a yawl. It has no sail and is a heavy, specially built boat designed for its particular type of duty. In the present Rules and Regulations it is referred to as a "boat" but in earlier regulations it was called "canoe" and was so termed by the pilots of forty years or so ago. To this generation of pilots it is a "yawl" which accounts for the quotation marks around that word in the text of this publication.

We should also like to call attention to the fact that while some awards for courage in saving victims of wrecks are mentioned in this volume, they do not represent all such awards to pilots but are only those about which we happened to learn in our research.

Ralph M. Eastman

Acknowledgments

In the preparation of this volume we had the wholehearted co-operation of the following: The Pilots of Boston, Clarence E. Doane, their Agent, and his assistant Paul H. Rauhaut, James L. Bruce of The Bostonian Society, Dennis A. Dooley, State Librarian, and his associates, Maynard H. Hutchinson, Collector of Customs, and members of his staff, the Archives Department of the Commonwealth, the Boston Public Library, the Peabody Museum, Salem, the Hyannis Public Library and the South Yarmouth Library. Also, we wish to thank George M. Cushing, Jr. of Boston for his fine work in photographing many of the paintings and other illustrations which appear in this volume.

Miss Katherine G. Rogers, Miss Alice G. Higgins and Miss Marion Lawless, of the Bank staff, deserve special mention for their devoted assistance to the author in the many details involved in the proof reading, typing and research required in compiling the material presented.

We also are indebted to the following persons, in addition to those mentioned in the text, for their helpfulness in our efforts to produce an interesting publication: Miss E. Florence Addison, Robert B. Applebee, George L. Barnes, Mrs. Ralph R. Barr, Mrs. Gladys Bond, M. V. Brewington, William E. Chamberlain, Theodore Chase, Captain Harold L. Colbeth, the late Patrick J. Connelly, Chas. H. P. Copeland, Edward Cunningham, Miss Irma L. Farris, Boston Postmaster J. P. W. Finn, Leo Flaherty, Dr. Henry S. Forbes, Guy E. Foster, the late Captain F. C. Gevalt, Russell Gerould, Sheldon S. Heap, Theodore K. Hebert, R. M. Hicks, Adams Sherman Hill, George F. Hines, Lawrence W. Jenkins, T. Edward Kellar, Mrs. Margaret Mann, Captain Clarence A. Martin, Miss Catherine R. McCarthy, J. J. McManus, Lawrence J. O'Connell, William E. Palmer, Frank H. Peterson, Mrs. Caroline R. Siebens, J. L. Van Steenburgh and the late Harold F. Wheeler.

It has been our custom *to prepare and distribute to our friends publications designed to prove enjoyable and of historical value to them. We trust that this 1956 brochure — the fortieth — will succeed in fulfilling this desire.*

We also hope the impression received will be so favorable the reader will feel that our publications typify the institution which issues them and that the high standard maintained in their form and material is characteristic of the banking and trust services we render.

It would be gratifying to us if the enjoyment derived from our brochures should induce readers to consider our bank when occasions arise for opening bank accounts, or taking advantage of our loaning facilities which are available to business organizations and individuals in domestic as well as foreign fields. We also welcome opportunities to be helpful in making small loans, including those financing the purchase of automobiles and household appliances.

It may be that some readers do not realize that our Trust Department is qualified by long experience to serve effectively as Agent in the handling of investments, as Trustee of Living Trusts, Pension and Profit Sharing Plans, Life Insurance Trusts, as Executor and Trustee under wills and in any other recognized trust capacity.

It will be a pleasure to us to furnish to those interested detailed information in regard to any of the various services which we render.

WILLIAM D. IRELAND
President

EDWARD L. BIGELOW
Chairman of the Board

Photograph by Fay Foto Service, Inc.

Pilot Melvin R. Jackson boarding the *S.S. City of Khartoum* via its Jacob's ladder, August 19, 1949. There is quite an art to getting hold of one of these ladders and climbing up the side of a ship, especially in a gale or when they are iced over.

TABLE OF CONTENTS

BOSTON HARBOR 1840

This reproduction of an early colored print shows how Boston appeared to an artist of that day. We have read that pilots at one period wore top hats, or "plug hats," as they were commonly called, and the rowboat in the left foreground could represent a pilot being rowed out by two apprentices but we have not been able to verify this.

BACKGROUND OF PILOTAGE

The casual looking pilot who comes aboard to take a great ocean liner into port is the successor to an honored heritage of courage, skill and responsibility.

Pilotage, an ancient and reputable calling, has been carried on ever since mariners first left their home ports to voyage to strange harbors. In those early days, "pilot" designated the man on a vessel who had charge of directing her course. Now, by general usage, the term is applied to a person, not attached to a vessel, who conducts it into or out of a harbor, or over shoals, or wherever navigation requires special local knowledge. Roman law prescribed that a shipmaster must employ a pilot when occasion required, or be responsible for ensuing damage. Maritime laws in various European countries imposed financial penalties and sometimes corporal punishment on the master if a pilot was not taken on when necessary and damages followed.

The word "pilot" comes from the old Dutch words "pijl" and "lood" meaning the sounding lead used by generations of pilots before the invention of the fathometer which is in general use today. The first known movement for an organized pilotage system as an aid to commerce is said to have taken place in Holland.

It is interesting to know that Amerigo Vespucci, early Italian explorer from whom America got its name, was appointed Chief Pilot, or Pilot Major, of Spain in 1508, responsible for the preparation of charts for the use of mariners and others. During his regime, orders were given that "henceforth all navigators sailing towards known or unknown parts of India, who should discover new regions, islands, harbors or bays, affording some interest for the general chart, should, on their return to Europe, report the same to the Chief Pilot." Sebastian Cabot, another early explorer of this country, reported his findings to Spain in 1512, in accordance with Vespucci's decree.

Later, in 1549, Edward VI appointed Cabot Grand Pilot of England. It will be seen in the chapter on the Boston Marine Society which appears in this brochure that the founders of that organization had a regulation somewhat similar to that of Vespucci in their original "Rules and Orders."

Getting closer to home, one of the earliest known pilots in New England waters was Squanto the Indian who was such a helpful friend of the Pilgrims. In 1622, he was taken on as pilot of the *Swan* by Governor Bradford who understood that the native knew how to thread the "deangerous shoulds & roring breakers" at the elbow of the Cape as he had been around that way twice before. He was also expected to act as interpreter for the Governor in negotiating for the food which they expected to purchase from the Monomoyick Indians who were not in a particularly friendly mood toward the white men just then. Unfortunately, Squanto's memory did not serve him too well, or perhaps there had been some major shifting of the sands since his previous trips. While his piloting apparently left something to be desired, the *Swan* arrived safely in Monomoyick Bay (Chatham) in due course. However, as an interpreter and peacemaker Squanto performed very well indeed as he succeeded in getting the natives into a sufficiently friendly state of mind so that they were willing to trade with Governor Bradford and his party. The results were goodly supplies of corn and beans for the Pilgrims. Unfortunately, soon after the arrival at Chatham, Squanto was stricken with a raging fever from which he died. Before he passed on, he bequeathed his few possessions to Bradford and other friends and besought the Governor to pray for him so that he might "go to ye Englishmens God in heaven."

Aviation, of course, within a comparatively short time has given a new meaning to the word "pilot" which is perhaps the first to come to mind when the word now is heard or seen.

The adoption of pilotage in our country derives historically from the establishment in 1514 of the Corporation of Trinity

House, commonly referred to as "Trinity House" in maritime circles. This was an association of mariners having its headquarters at Deptford in Kent, England, which was made a royal dockyard by Henry VIII, where outgoing ships were supplied with pilots by the corporation. Later, headquarters were moved to London. "Trinity House" is still an honored body having charge, directly or indirectly, of most of the lighthouses, buoys and pilotage services of Great Britain.

In Massachusetts the earliest information we could find of official action in regard to pilotage was the law passed by the Commonwealth in July of 1783 authorizing the Governor, with advice of his Council, to appoint suitable persons as pilots for the several harbors of Boston, Salem, Marblehead, Gloucester, Newburyport, Plymouth, Nantucket, Martha's Vineyard "and other places as may become necessary;" each pilot "to have Branches or Warrants, and to be under oath and enter into bonds of £1000 for the due performance of the trust reposed in him." The following are those who were appointed to that trust for the harbors of Boston, the Vineyard and Nantucket Shoals:

For the harbor of Boston
Thomas **Knox** and **Robert** Knox
For the Vineyard and Nantucket Shoals
Samuel Daggett, John Holmes, William Daggett,
Abner Norton, David Norton, James Shaw,
Lemuel Kelly, Francis Norton, Abisha Pease,
Isaac Daggett

The colonists, from their experience in England and elsewhere, appreciated the need of competent pilots and some form of regulation of pilotage. Their regulations were in operation when our nation came into being. Though the right to regulate interstate and foreign commerce was given to the United States by the Constitution, the regulation of pilotage was left with the States.

Courtesy of the Consulate of The Netherlands, Boston

Monument to Frans Naerebout,
said to be the first professional pilot.

This monument erected in honor of Naerebout stands in Bellamypark, Vlissingen (Flushing), The Netherlands. He announced himself as prepared to take the sailing vessels of his day in and out of the harbors of Holland which he had studied carefully until he was familiar with all danger spots. The inscription, translated into English, reads "Frans Naerebout, 1748–1818, Heroic Saver of Shipwrecked, Skillful Seaman, Undaunted Pilot." There is a fund named in his honor, administered from headquarters at The Hague, for the benefit of relatives of the maritime staff and the militarized pilotage staff who lost their lives due to disaster during the mobilization of 1914–1919. It was designed, also, to extend support to members of the maritime staff who lost their ability, partly or in whole, to provide for a living.

WHY TAKE ON A PILOT?

Many seafaring voyagers and others have probably won-
dered why, after having brought his craft safely over thousands
of miles of frequently turbulent water, it was necessary for
an experienced master of a great ocean liner to take on a pilot
at the entrance of a harbor to guide his ship for a short distance
farther into port. When one stops to think, the answer is
rather simple. Special training and experience in the science
of navigation are required, of course, to conduct a vessel across
the sea. Accurate and up-to-date knowledge of the details of
a harbor, its aids to navigation and its hazards, is necessary to
bring a vessel safely and expeditiously into port. Navigating
a narrow, congested, tidal-current channel, day or night and
during periods of low visibility and rough weather, plus
locating desired anchorage, demands the services of a local
expert. It is not fair to expect the master of a ship to be
familiar with all the special hazards of each harbor into which
he brings his vessel. Experienced masters of ocean liners realize
that a ship is generally safer on the open sea than she is
when along a coast or in a busy harbor.

An editorial in the "Quincy Patriot Ledger" a few years
ago seems to treat this subject so well that we have obtained
permission to quote from it here:

"A ship's master is perfectly at home from pilot boat to
pilot boat; that is, when he is on the high seas. But when
he approaches the land or enters a harbor, he often is in need
— in grave need — of local knowledge, knowledge as to depths,
shoals, channels, lights, buoys, tides.

"He gets this information from the pilot he takes with
him on entering or leaving a port.

"On the advice of the pilot, practically speaking, depends
the safety of a ship and cargo, often worth many millions of

dollars; and the lives and safety of her ship's company." From the above it is easy to understand why one seasoned Captain remarked that of all the people who boarded his ship there were none more worthy than the pilot of the customary greeting, "Glad to have you aboard."

The present well-regulated system of compulsory pilotage for American vessels engaged in foreign trade and for all foreign-flag vessels entering the port of Boston is similar to that maintained in practically every port of the world. As far as we have been able to find, whenever this system has been discontinued in a port of any importance it has always been restored, generally on petition of merchants and insurance and shipping interests. Marine underwriters have always endorsed the system and failure to employ a pilot, when procurable, is likely to be taken as evidence of negligence on the part of the master of a vessel involved in an accident in a harbor.

"Compulsory" is not a popular word generally but in this case it seems logical and reasonable to have sound laws and regulations which must be followed carefully in order to maintain reliable, responsible service of the nature required. Long and bitter experience by practical business and shipping men brought about this development in pilotage designed for the preservation of lives and property, as well as prevention of accidents which might blockade a channel and bottle up harbor traffic for hours or days.

As a matter of fact, when we compare the traffic rules in the harbor to those on the highways, we become conscious at once of the fact that the regulations to prevent accidents and save lives on land are also compulsory, as well as numerous. Instead of lights and buoys we are warned by those familiar signs "No Passing," "Soft Shoulder," "Dangerous Curves," "Stop" and numerous directional signs and varying speed limit markers. If we do not heed them we are likely to be informed by an officer of the law that penalties are involved when they are ignored. Efforts are made to engineer safety into highways but we still need compulsory laws and regulations to protect us from our own rashness and carelessness. Also, in Massachusetts we have compulsory automobile insurance. It would be unwise and fatal to let individuals drive at any speed they desired, — passing and turning out, without restriction, on the highways where dangers are generally visible. The same applies to the movement of large craft on the waters of a busy harbor where most of the hazards are out of sight. The Harbor Police of Boston watch the behavior of all craft in the harbor, as outlined briefly at the end of this chapter.

While pilotage may be requested by masters of craft of any size, foreign vessels under 350 tons register which decline pilotage when offered by a pilot boat on station are liable to one-half of the regular pilotage fees. Vessels plying the coastwise trade and naval vessels are exempt from compulsory payment of pilotage but, of course, they may request the service and pay the regular fees. These fees, by the way, are based on the draught of vessels and are established by the Massachusetts Legislature as fair and proper. There are some other exceptions but it is not our intention to go into too much detail here which might not interest the majority of our readers.

In addition to the use of the service being compulsory, it may be said that the duties of the Boston pilots are compulsory as well. They are required to follow the laws as laid down by the Commonwealth of Massachusetts, and to observe the rules established by the Pilot Commissioners including those in regard to being available day and night and in all kinds of weather. If a pilot disobeys, he is liable to suspension or revocation of his commission.

It is up to the pilots to keep a sharp lookout for vessels inward bound or they may be subject to complaint or loss of revenue, or both. The law says that if a vessel liable to pilotage arrives within a line drawn from Harding's Ledge to the Graves and thence to Nahant Head, without having been offered the services of a pilot, it is exempt from payment of pilotage fees, unless such services are requested. A pilot boat, being on its station and displaying the signals required by law, is considered as having made an offer of pilotage service. The established pilot signal by day is a white and blue flag, white next the mast; by night a white light over a red light at the mast head, visible all around the horizon.

Years ago when craft of 200 tons or over were required to take pilotage on entering Boston Harbor, or pay the pilotage fee, it is said that the owners of one fleet of barks used as freighters had these constructed to register 199 tons, thus avoiding the pilotage charge.

In the case of vessels returning from sea in consequence of head winds, stress of weather, or damage, compulsory pilotage does not apply.

Photograph by one of Boston's most noted early photographers,
N. L. Stebbins.

The Boston waterfront police force was established in 1853 and consisted of two patrolmen and the rowboat pictured above equipped with a leg-o'-mutton sail. Now, from Police Station No. 8 at 521 Commercial Street, under the direction of the Harbor Master, who is a member of the Boston Police Department, this Division carries out its many duties with a

staff of 43 officers and men and has five powered craft ranging from 16 feet to 60 feet in length. It has jurisdiction over
an area comprising 46.1 square miles of land, including islands,
and 50.7 square miles of water, extending to the three mile
limit.

The Harbor Master among his other duties is responsible
for regulating the anchorage of vessels and has to see that every
vessel from a foreign port is supplied with a copy of the official
Harbor regulations. To keep the "parking" problem under
control in the harbor, he may, at the expense of the master
or owners, cause the removal of any vessel which is not moved
when so directed by him, just as illegal parkers of automobiles
may find their cars towed away by the police on land. The
harbor is patrolled day and night to see that regulations are
obeyed and to prevent any craft from being operated in a reck-
less manner. The present Harbor Master is Lieutenant James
J. Crowley.

*   *   *

OUT IN HURRICANE CAROL

Captain James E. Frye who has been a pilot of Boston
harbor since 1943 had a rare experience during Hurricane
Carol on August 31, 1954. He had been put aboard the
Sagoland of the Swedish Orient Line on her approach to the
harbor when the first fury of the hurricane struck. The ship's
anchors could not hold and, to quote Captain Rolf Bauer, her
master: "it was only by the expert seamanship and skillful
shiphandling under extreme conditions, with heavy rain, low
visibility and wind gusts of 110 knots, that Captain Frye kept
the ship from being blown ashore." The buffeting lasted
over three hours and a half and during that time the ship could
not be docked. Captain Frye had to jockey her about in
rather restricted space until the hurricane abated when she
was finally tied up to her dock. Shortly afterwards, a letter
was received from the ship's owners commending the pilot
highly for his outstanding service.

THE MAKING OF A PILOT

Competent pilotage is recognized as an essential and valuable factor in maritime commerce, but comparatively few realize what prolonged and serious training is necessary to assure that the pilots of Boston Harbor will be qualified to discharge their important responsibilities.

In order to be eligible for training, a young man must be a native born, or naturalized, citizen of the United States, between the ages of 17 and 25, of good character and in first-class physical condition. Before he can take the pilot examinations, he must serve an apprenticeship which usually runs from six to ten years. During this period, the candidate serves as Boatkeeper, eventually advancing to First Boatkeeper, and becomes an expert in handling, particularly in bad weather, the "yawls" in which the pilots are rowed from the pilot boat to the vessels they are to board. These 14 foot boats are especially designed for the rugged treatment involved in their use which is so important in the work of the pilots. Through all the years, no perfect way has been discovered to get a pilot safely to and from a vessel in the open sea. The New York pilots use power boats but the Boston pilots still continue to rely on the tried-and-true sturdy rowboat, powered by two boatmen apprentices. While getting a lot of physical exercise in handling the "yawl" and learning the duties of a Boatkeeper, the embryo pilot carries on his studies of navigation, seamanship, local and Federal pilotage regulations, and other subjects essential to his calling. He also gradually becomes familiar with the location of landmarks and aids to navigation such as lighthouses, beacons, and buoys, as well as acquiring knowledge as to where to steer clear of dangerous hidden reefs and other obstructions which may menace the safety of shipping in the Harbor.

In respect to that last sentence, it is amusing to recall the story of an aspirant for a pilot's license (not at Boston) who was undergoing his oral test. The examiner asked him if he knew where all the sand bars were in the waters where he was to perform his duties if granted a commission. His reply was: "No, I don't." "Then how in the world do you expect to do any piloting?" was the next question, tartly put. "Because I know where they ain't," was the winning reply.

With years of training behind him, a Boston candidate, if he has served at least one year as First Boatkeeper from the time he was registered as such in the office of the Pilot Commissioners and three years as Second or Third Boatkeeper, may apply for a commission as a Boston pilot. There are a few more requirements to be met before taking his examinations. Of course, there must be a vacancy in the roster of 24 pilots. He must be recommended by the Executive Committee of the Boston Pilots' Association, and approved by the Trustees of the Boston Marine Society. He must also have served an intensive probationary period of not less than three months under a commissioned pilot on inward and outward bound vessels of various draughts. This is called the "riding period" by the pilots.

The examinations are designed to prove that the candidate is "thoroughly posted on the direction of the Current, Courses, Distances, Obstructions, Aids to Navigation and depth of water in all Channels, Inland and International Rules of the Road, Safe handling of all classes of Vessels and be familiar with the Magnetic and Gyro Compass," to quote from the official Rules and Regulations for the Port of Boston. After successfully passing such tests, a commission is granted him as Warrant Pilot, allowing him for the next twelve months to pilot ships of 18 feet draught. During the following year he can pilot those of 20 feet draught. At the expiration of two years from the date of his first commission, if all goes well, he becomes a Full Branch Pilot and thenceforth is addressed as

"Captain." On obtaining this final commission, all restrictions are removed and he can pilot a ship of any draught into or out of port. Boston pilots also must hold Federal pilot licenses for Boston Harbor and its approaches. One legal requirement, not mentioned so far, is that before receiving a commission he must file with the State Treasurer a bond of $1000, conditioned on the faithful performance of his duties and the payment of any damages accruing from his negligence, unskillfulness or unfaithfulness.

It will be seen that the responsibilities of piloting are taken very seriously in Boston Harbor. This is the result of long experience which years ago demonstrated the necessity of fostering a group of reliable men, thoroughly trained to render pilotage service of the highest quality, who can be depended upon to be on duty at all times in all kinds of weather. Naturally the rewards have to be fair and attractive in order to maintain the continuity of such a group of men by making it desirable to promising youths to undertake the long training and study involved in meeting the exacting requirements of the life of a pilot and to assume the serious obligations inherent in such a career.

The present arrangement seems to give general satisfaction to all concerned and it is all accomplished without expense to the Commonwealth.

The reference earlier in this chapter to "Rules of the Road" brings to mind the following anecdote, obviously of overseas origin, which seems to point up the need for expert pilotage. During a dense fog, the officer on the bridge of a large vessel was becoming more and more apprehensive. As he leaned over the rail of the bridge, trying to pierce the gloom, he saw a hazy figure leaning on a rail a few yards away. Almost choking with exasperation, he yelled: "What do you think you're doing with your blinking ship? Don't you know the rules of the road?" An unruffled voice replied: "This ain't no blinkin' ship, guv'nor. This 'ere's a lighthouse."

PILOT BOAT ROSEWAY, WINTER OF 1947

Pilot Captains Malcolm A. MacDonald and Stanley R. Balcom in bow of the *Roseway*.

Left to right: Cook John Melanson, Engineer David Lowry, Boatmen Charles Crocker, Robert Cleverly, Shelton Collins (#1 Boatman), Captain Stanley R. Balcom, Irving Gardner, James Chambers and Captain Malcolm A. MacDonald, *Roseway*, 1947.

"Yawl" IN ACTION

This picture showing a "yawl" from the pilot boat *North-ern Light* in action was taken in 1940 by Arthur Griffin, nationally-known photographer.   In the foreground is appren-tice William H. Lewis, Jr., then of Braintree and later of Barn-stable, Mass.   Young "Bill" became a pilot in due course and on January 11, 1954, at the age of 40, met a tragic death when the "yawl" of the pilot boat *Pilot* capsized while on the way to put him aboard the navy tanker *Kennebago*.   A terrific north-east storm of near-blizzard proportions was lashing the southern New England coast at the time.   Also lost was apprentice Ernest W. Grundy, Jr., of Arlington.   Miraculously rescued was apprentice John P. Cushman, 3rd, of Winthrop.   In trying to haul Cushman aboard the *Pilot,* Llewellyn W. McMilan, 60, of Brighton, the oldest pilot then in service, was stricken with a heart attack and died.   Others aboard the *Pilot* who aided in the rescue of Cushman and in the heroic attempt to reach Lewis and Grundy, were Justus A. Bailey, Richard S. Woodman, Robert Murphy, Lee Auger, David Lowry, Frank Harriman and Irving Gardner.   Joseph I. Cordes, Jr., now a pilot, is the apprentice boatman in the background of the illustration.

Courtesy Captain William G. Jenkins

A RARE BIT OF PILOTAGE

The photograph reproduced above was taken by Captain Jenkins who piloted the huge Texas Tower out of Boston Harbor July 12, 1955 on its way to its permanent location 110 miles off Cape Cod. This was the first of a series of U. S. offshore radar outposts to be set up along the Atlantic coast to warn against enemy attacks. It required five tugs to get the 6000 ton Tower out of the Bethlehem Steel Company's East Boston ship yard and two sea-going tugs to take it to its destination. Captain Jenkins did the piloting from one of these two tugs. The picture shows the pilot boat *Pilot* maneuvering near the Tower. Captain Jenkins is a son-in-law of one of the long-time members of the Bank's staff, now on retirement, Arthur Keach.

THE BOSTON MARINE SOCIETY

This Society, the oldest of its kind in the world, has been a very important factor in maintaining efficient and dependable pilotage in Boston Harbor.

No story about pilotage locally would be complete if it did not call attention to a few, at least, of the Society's activities undertaken on behalf of safe navigation and pilot training.

The organization is the outgrowth of an association of sea captains which "began at Boston in New England, June 1, 1742" under the name of "The Fellowship Club." Later, the name was changed to "Marine Society" and on February 2, 1754, "in the twenty-seventh year of the reign of our sovereign lord, George the Second, of Great Britain, France and Ireland, king, defender of the faith, . . ." the Society was incorporated by a charter granted by "William Shirley, Esqr., Captain General and Governor-in-Chief in and over His Majesty's Province of the Massachusetts Bay in New England, and Vice-Admiral of the same and of the Maritime Parts thereto adjoining." The charter states that the principal ends of the Society were "to improve the knowledge of this coast by their several members upon their arrival from sea, communicating their observations inwards and outwards of the variations of the needle, the soundings, courses and distances, and all other remarkable things about it in writing, to be lodged with the Society for the making of the navigation more safe; and also to relieve one another and their families in poverty and other adverse accidents in life." The change to the present name — Boston Marine Society — occurred when the powers of incorporation were enlarged by act of the General Court of our Commonwealth in the year 1809.

For many years the Society had the whole management of pilotage in Boston Harbor. From 1783 to 1836 the Trustees of the Society acted as Pilot Commissioners, spending the Society's money and giving their time without compensation. In 1836 they asked to be relieved of these duties and the Commonwealth enacted a law making the Trustees of the Society the third party to act with two Commissioners. In 1855 the Society retired from this work and control of pilotage was placed in the hands of the Governor and Council. After seven years' trial this was found unsatisfactory and in 1862, on the united request of merchants, underwriters, ship owners, shipmasters and pilots, supervision of pilotage was put back into the hands of the Trustees of the Society where it has remained ever since.

The two Pilot Commissioners for Boston Harbor are now nominated by the Trustees of the Society and are appointed by the Governor and Council. This has resulted in the appointment as Commissioners of well qualified nautical men who have not only officiated as pilots but who, also, as shipmasters, have engaged the services of pilots in various ports. Another favorable result has been the selection of a body of efficient pilots, considered among the best in the nation. The Trustees of the Society fix the compensation of the Pilot Commissioners and their allowances for office rent, clerk hire and incidental expenses, which are paid out of the amounts turned over to the Commissioners by the pilots. The present Commissioners are Odber R. Farrell of Belmont and Charles T. Snow of Brookline.

To go back to 1742, according to the "Rules and Orders to be observed by a *loving* and *friendly* SOCIETY called THE FELLOWSHIP CLUB," monthly meetings were to be held at the Sun Tavern, or such other public houses in Boston as the Society agreed upon. In those days, of course, taverns were the usual places for holding meetings of this sort. The records show that The Fellowship Club and its successors met at various times at the British, American and Exchange Coffee Houses as well as at the Crown and Bunch of Grapes Taverns. The last-named was located at the corner of King Street and

Mackerel Lane, (now State and Kilby Streets) part of the present site of the State Street Office of our Bank.

One of the original "Rules" on which the present by-laws of the Society are based contained the provision that "such Member or Members as shall go a Voyage to sea and shall Return Successful, without being Cast-away, taken by the Enemy, or meeting with any other Misfortune, shall pay *Six Pence* Sterling into the Box for the Use of the Society for each and every month he shall have been absent." On the other hand, if he suffered any of the dire misfortunes mentioned, he was excused from paying *Six Pence* Sterling, monthly, for the time he was absent and could be "Relieved according to the Nature of his Misfortune and the Ability of the Box." Now, to explain "The Box!" Funds for relief work were provided in those early days by monthly payments from members and such payments were dropped into an unlocked brass-bound, wood and leather chest which is still preserved and which has always been known as "The Box." This may well have been the genesis of marine insurance and organized aid to the needy in America.

Membership in The Fellowship Club had been restricted to "such Persons only, who are now, or have been Commanders of Vessels." In due course, however, after the change in the name of the organization as previously mentioned, it was decided that shipping executives and others especially interested in maritime affairs might well be admitted as honorary members. The most notable of those admitted in the early days was John Adams, who later earned his place in history as the second President of the United States. His long interest in developing a strong navy for our nation provided a sound basis for his eligibility for such membership. Another President, Franklin D. Roosevelt, on July 11, 1933, was elected a *marine* member of the Society, qualifying by his long experience in sailing. Many prominent New England merchants, bankers and lawyers have been elected honorary members.   One of these was the late Allan Forbes whose grandfather, Robert Bennet Forbes, was president of the Society from 1844 to 1846.

To this day the Society has continued its two main objectives.   Methods have changed considerably but the relief work is still carried out with great care and consideration.   The purpose of "making of the navigation more safe" has been forwarded by advocating the installation of adequate safeguards to navigation and the Society has been a tower of strength to Boston and the Commonwealth in its supervision of pilotage, which contributes so much to safety in the Harbor.

*   *   *

That the dangers of piloting were not always confined to the fury of angry winds and waves is shown in a clipping from the Boston "Globe" dated November 20, 1899.   This records the fact that two boatkeepers on the *Adams* #4, under Capt. Watson S. Dolliver, were badly injured by the accidental discharge of a 6-pounder gun with which they were signalling an incoming vessel during a dense fog.   The men were given first aid by army surgeons at Fort Warren and then were taken to Long Island Hospital for treatment.   First Boatkeeper Charles W. Frye, who lost a finger in the blast, later became a pilot.   The *Adams* was built for Capt. John H. Jeffery in 1888 by Moses Adams at Essex, Mass. and was named for a prominent Bostonian, Melvin O. Adams, we understand, not for her builder.   She was designed by the noted naval architect Edward Burgess who also designed three America's Cup defenders, the *Puritan* in 1885, the *Mayflower* in 1886 and the *Volunteer* in 1887.   The *Adams* was in the pilotage service for several years and was kept as a reserve boat when the new regulations went into effect in 1901.   Later she was sold and went into the Portuguese immigrant trade, being sunk eventually by the Germans during World War I.

Photographed by George M. Cushing, Jr.

Courtesy of Mrs. Nina Fletcher Little

OVERMANTEL PANEL
Painted by Jonathan Welch Edes, 1789

PILOTS AT BOSTON LIGHT

The rare panel painted by Jonathan Welch Edes in 1789, reproduced on the previous page, was removed from an old house in Chelsea, Massachusetts, which was demolished some years ago. It is now in the collection of Mrs. Nina Fletcher Little and we are very much pleased to be permitted to include it in this volume. Boston Light appears in the background and in the foreground is a "yawl" in which a pilot is being rowed to an incoming ship.

Boston Light was the first erected in the United States following an order passed by the General Court of Massachusetts that "a Light-House be Erected at the charge of this Province at the entrance of the Harbour of Boston." The location selected for the lighthouse was on that part of the Great Brewster called "Beacon Island." It is, in effect, a separate island joined to the Great Brewster by a bar which is exposed to view at low water. Since the establishment of the light, the island has generally been called "Lighthouse Island" and it so appears on present Government charts of the harbor. Before 1715 it was also known as the Little Brewster though that name appears on some maps made earlier, as well as later, for the island now designated as the Outer Brewster. The lighthouse was illuminated for the first time on September 14, 1716. The first keeper, George Worthylake, was a pilot engaged for the sum of £50 per year which was augmented by his fees as one of the pilots of Boston Harbor.

The Act for the erection of the lighthouse provided that there should "be paid to the receiver of the Impost [the keeper of the Light] by the Master of all Ships and Vessells Except Coasters the Duty of one penny per Tun Inwards and also one penny per Tun outwards and no more for every Tun of the burthen of said Vessell before they load or unlade the goods therein." Until taken over by the United States Government in 1790 the expenses of the lighthouse were defrayed by this duty upon vessels, which came to be known as "light money." Fishing vessels and vessels engaged in bringing lumber, stone, etc. from ports within the Province were required to pay but 5 shillings a year. The Act expressly defined the meaning of the word "coasters," provided for the measurement of vessels and the collection of the tax, and stated that a person should be appointed from time to time "by the General Court or Assembly" to be the keeper of the light. As major repairs had to be made, the fees were raised for periods of from two to three years to cover such additional expenses.

Lighthouse Island continued to be used as an outpost for pilots for several years. From this vantage point they kept a lookout for incoming vessels and were always on hand to respond to a signal for their services.

Unfortunately the first two keepers of the Light, Worthylake and his successor in 1718, Captain John Hayes, also a pilot, were drowned — not while carrying out their official duties but while boating elsewhere. Robert Saunders might be listed as the third keeper but he served only a day or so until the newly appointed successor to Captain Hayes, pilot Robert Ball, could take over the responsibilities of keeper. Appointed in 1733, Ball served for forty years and had his troubles.

In due course he became greatly incensed as there seemed to be a growing practice, while he was busy with his lighthouse activities, for interlopers in small craft, especially in the summer time, to take pilotage away from him and also to usurp his duty of collecting fees from all vessels passing the Light, thereby collecting considerable sums. This practice was ended after he petitioned the authorities in 1739 to be appointed the *established* pilot of Boston Harbor. In his petition he stated that he had piloted vessels in winter time and charged no more than in the summer season, also that he had frequently been obliged to board vessels infected with small-pox to pilot them to the Province Hospital. Captain Hayes, Ball's predecessor as keeper, had complained earlier that during the summer almost every fisherman or boatman would act as pilot.

Ball's plea was successful and he was appointed the *established* pilot for three years, a maximum was fixed for his charges and elaborate provisions were made in his behalf. He was to keep two well-fitted boats and distinguish them from all others by having them painted white "down to the wale." The boat plying in the Bay was to fly a "broad blew Vane" at the masthead and the boat plying in the harbor a "broad red Vane." Anyone who imitated these distinguishing features was made liable to a fine of £5 to be recovered by Ball for his own use. If he or his agent went aboard a vessel before she got to the lighthouse and found another person in charge as pilot, Ball could claim half the fee.

The lighthouse having been destroyed during the Revolutionary War, the Boston Marine Society, ever watchful of the best interests of harbor navigation, addressed a memorial to the General Court in June of 1783 concerning the erection of a new lighthouse and "the Establishment of a regular, skillful System of Pilotage." As a result of this and of urging from other quarters, the Light was restored to service late in that year with Thomas Knox, Branch Pilot for the Port of Boston, as keeper.

In February 1789 an article written by Knox appeared in the "Massachusetts Magazine." An illustration with the story showed a pilot looking through a spy glass out to sea. One of the items in the collection in the Trust Department at our State Street Office, loaned to us by Dr. and Mrs. Franklin E. Campbell, is the first pilot commission issued by the Commonwealth of Massachusetts. It was granted to this same Thomas Knox under date of August 20, 1783, and bears the famous signature of John Hancock, as Governor.

When the lighthouse was turned over to the federal government in 1790, Knox declared that by accepting a commission as keeper from the President, he lost the friendship of Governor Hancock who gave the office of "Branch Pilot" to another.

It is said the early keepers regarded the title of "pilot" as a greater distinction than that of "lighthouse keeper."

The painter of the colorful panel reproduced here also painted a banner which was carried by the Marine Society, led by Captain Dunn, in the grand parade in Boston on October 24, 1789, to honor George Washington when he visited our city in his first year as President. Items in contemporary newspapers, "The Independent Chronicle and Universal Advertiser" and "The Massachusetts Centinel," indicate that the Marine Society had a prominent part in this event. All masters of vessels within the Town of Boston were requested "to meet at the Bunch of Grapes Tavern on the morning of the arrival of the President, there to form and fall into the Procession immediately after the Marine Society, agreeable to the Request of the Town." One item in the printed bulletin of instructions to participants in the parade was "The Marine Society is desired to appoint some person to arrange and accompany the seamen." This was done by way of a notice in "The Independent Chronicle" reading as follows: "The Mates and Seamen are desired to assemble [on the morning of the arrival of the President] on board the *Massachusetts Indiaman,* at the Governour's Wharf; there the Captains, Job Prince and Allen Hallet, will attend to arrange them, agreeable to a Vote of the Marine Society." In the official "Order of the Procession" the Marine Society was listed high up in the line of march "preceded by Captain Dunn with a flag, the device: *A ship passing the Light-house and a boat going to her."* The illustration on the banner was obviously similar to that on the panel. We cannot tell which came first, the panel or the banner, but probably the former. They were both painted in the same year when the subject was fresh in his mind and it is likely that the time element induced Edes to duplicate the view painted earlier that year rather than create a new one for the parade.

ISLAND NAMED FOR A PILOT

While Gallups Island in Boston Harbor is so recorded on the official charts of the U. S. Government, it was given its name because its first owner was Captain John Gallop, a noted Boston pilot, and is most commonly referred to locally as "Gallop's Island." On this island Captain Gallop had a snug farm, also a meadow on Long Island, a sheep pasture on Nix's Mate and a house in Boston. He was said to have been better acquainted with the harbor than any other man of his time. In 1633 he piloted the ship *Griffin* into Boston Harbor when Rev. John Cotton and Elder Thomas Leverett were among its passengers. He gained fame when, in 1636, after a desperate encounter off Block Island he recovered a vessel which had been taken by the Narragansett Indians from his friend John Oldham whom they had killed. This is supposed to be the first engagement that ever occurred between the inhabitants of the American colonies and enemies afloat.

In 1677, a vessel anchored off Gallups Island was found to have victims of smallpox on board. Unsuspecting people from the coast boarded her and soon the disease had spread in Massachusetts, taking the lives of about a thousand persons. This taught the people of the colony the need of strict quarantine regulations and the island was chosen as a quarantine station. In 1867 the federal government purchased the island and continued the quarantine operations there until August 30, 1937. All passengers were examined for disease by doctors from this island and if found afflicted with a contagious malady they were hospitalized there. Over the years the island was used to good advantage, harboring servicemen during four wars, caring for immigrants, and for the aged and infirm of Boston. In later years most of the work on the island consisted of fumigating vessels to get rid of rats which could bring disease into the country. The crews were taken off while the fumigation was taking place and were given medical examination.

Since August 30, 1937, quarantine operations have been carried out from headquarters in the U.S. Custom House at Boston. Instead of stopping at a quarantine station for inspection by port physicians and nurses, incoming passenger vessels now notify the authorities by radio if there are any cases of communicable disease aboard. If not, they, as well as all vessels in foreign trade, proceed directly to their docks where Quarantine Inspectors board them, thus eliminating much of the delay required previously which generally seemed interminable to passengers eager to get ashore.

*   *   *

"King's Handbook of Boston Harbor" published in 1889 by M. F. Sweetser gives a description of pilot boats which seems worthy of quotation here: "Hence the shapely pilot-boats are seen, cruising out and in, and toward the capes, in their fair symmetry meriting the eulogy of an officer of the Royal Navy: 'Our ingenious friends, the Americans, have contrived a set of pilot-boats which are the delight of every sailor. . . . They are truly 'water-witches,' for while they look so delicate and fragile that one feels at first as if the most moderate breeze must brush them from the face of the ocean, and scatter to the winds all their gay drapery, they can and do defy, as a matter of habit and choice, the most furious gales with which the rugged seaboard of America is visited in February and March.'"

Courtesy of Mrs. Allan Forbes

The *SYLPH*, Yacht and Pilot Boat, 1834–1851

The painting reproduced above was given to Allan Forbes by Charles H. Taylor many years ago. It seems especially appropriate to include it here as it was Mr. Taylor who suggested the subject for this brochure and Mr. Forbes who launched the author on its preparation.

The *SYLPH,* Yacht and Pilot Boat, 1834–1851

Speedy craft were essential to the pilots in the early com-
petitive days of piloting when they often had thrilling races for
the "prize" of bringing in a vessel from a foreign port. This
accounts for the fact that several yachts, noted for fast sailing,
were purchased by the pilots for their work.

One of the earliest to find its way to the piloting service
was the *Sylph* owned by Robert Bennet Forbes, grandfather
of Allan Forbes. Built in Boston in 1834 by Whitmore & Hol-
brook, for John P. Cushing, her construction was superintended
by Commodore Forbes. In her first and second seasons she was
used as a yacht and in 1835 sailed in the first recorded yacht
race in America, which will be described later.

The story of her purchase by Commodore Forbes seems
interesting enough to quote from his Memoirs: "We arrived,
(with Messrs. Cushing, S. Cabot, R. D. Shepherd and others
aboard) at Woods Hole in good time when Governor Swain of
Naushon came aboard and offered to pilot us through 'Lone
Rock' passage where the tide rushes through like a mill race.
Our pilot, Sylvanus Dagett said it would not be safe but Mr.
Cushing concluded to try it. The breeze was fresh and all went
well until we had got by 'Lone Rock' when the tide caught her
and she went on the ledge opposite the 'Lone Rock.' At the
moment I saw the cutter *Hamilton,* Captain W. A. Howard, in
the sound, bound West. I fired a gun and lowered our flag and
Howard instantly came and anchored as near as was safe. Our
ballast was taken out and finally the *Sylph* was floated. Captain Howard hove her out and smoothed the broken false keel
and the copper. While she was on the rock with one end out
of the water and the other submerged, Mr. Cushing proposed
to sell her by auction and she was knocked off to me for about
one fourth of her cost."

From a painting by Charles J. A. Wilson

Courtesy of the Pilots of Boston

PILOT BOAT *NORTHERN LIGHT*

Approaching one of the ships of the United Fruit Company's "Great White Fleet."

It was on the return trip, on August 3, 1835 that the race referred to took place and again we quote Commodore Forbes: "As we opened out Holmes' Hole, we saw the *Wave* at anchor and immediately hauled up for her and, passing near I jumped on board. Commodore John C. Stevens and his guests were at breakfast; I invited him to a trial of speed to Newport and we were soon under way, running down towards West Chop and while in smooth water the *Wave* gained rapidly but when we got nearly up to Tarpaulin Cove the sea became rough and it soon became apparent that the *Sylph* was gaining. I had remained on board the *Wave* and watched every movement of both boats; it soon became certain that the *Sylph* was gaining and Commodore Stevens concluded to bear away and wait in Tarpaulin Cove for better weather." On this occasion the *Sylph* was skippered by William C. Fowler of the Boston pilot service.

In August, 1935, in honor of this early yacht race, due we understand to the initiative of William V. Swan, Yachting Editor of the "Boston Globe," the one hundredth anniversary was marked by a Centennial Race held off Martha's Vineyard. Sponsored by the Southern Massachusetts Yacht Racing Association, the race was held in very nearly the exact waters and almost at the very hour of the first race between the *Sylph* and the *Wave*. The race was open to all cruising yachts, sailing in two divisions — the first for those 45 to 73 feet overall; and the second for those between 30 and 45 feet. Two handsome silver bowls were offered as prizes by the descendants of Commodores Forbes and Stevens, the two rival owners of the contending yachts in the original race. A great-grandson and namesake of Commodore Forbes participated in this anniversary race on a Forbes boat.

The *Sylph* was used as a pilot boat in Boston Harbor in 1836 and 1837, being sold to the Sandy Hook pilots in October of 1837, and registered at Newark, where she was owned. She was lost in the winter of 1851, with all hands, during a terrific blizzard off Barnegat, New Jersey.

In 1834, according to Commodore Forbes, the only other yacht of note was the *Northern Light* owned by Col. W. P. Winchester. Singularly enough, a pilot boat put into commission by the Boston Pilots in 1934 — just 100 years later — was named the *Northern Light* and had been built at Oakland, California, in 1927 as a yacht for John Borden, a Chicago banker. Designed for Arctic service, her owner took her into the far North on an expedition for the Field Museum of Chicago. Her stout hull of heavy oak was strengthened from water line to keel with a shielding of ironwood that enabled her to cope with heavy ice without fear of damage. She was in Boston pilot service from 1934 until 1941 when she was sold to the United States Army for use on an unannounced mission. While she was on duty in Boston as a pilot boat, one of her distinguished guests was Charles Francis Adams, former Secretary of the Navy and later Chairman of the Board of the State Street Trust Company. He was very much interested in the description of her stout construction and inspected her thoroughly.

While on the subject of yachts, it may be news to some of our readers that the famous yacht *America* — winner of the first international yacht race in 1851 — was sailed by Captain Richard Brown of New Jersey, a Sandy Hook pilot. He took her across the Atlantic to win the now famed America's Cup. He followed his profession as a pilot for many years after this great victory, ending his career in the winter of 1884 as a result of infection after having his feet badly frostbitten in the course of duty.

Another yacht of the early days which found its way into pilot service was the *Coquette* which is described in the next chapter.

PILOT BOAT FLEET 1859

The scene on the next page is from a wood cut in "Ballou's Pictorial" of 1859 based on a pencil drawing by Alfred Waud. It is unusual as it portrays all but one of the pilot boat fleet at that time. The one missing is the *Bouquet,* #4, a new boat which had not joined the fleet when the drawing was made. Our research turned up the numbers of three shown in the illustration — *Syren,* #1, *Phantom,* #5 and *Wm. Starkey,* #6. The other two are the *Coquette* and the *Friend.* A story which accompanied the picture stated in part: "These boats are all well-built, of exquisite model and crack sailers, and are manned by as fine a set of men as ever trod a deck or handled a sheet. They ride the waves like sea-ducks, and with their hardy crews are constantly exposed to the roughest weather." The friendly and enthusiastic writer ended the story as follows: "The pilot boats are the trimmest craft in our waters, and they are handled with a dexterity which only long professional experience can give. They are decked over, and in a heavy seaway their decks are constantly wet. In good hands they are perfect life boats, and are capable of making a voyage around the world. The skill of the best builders has been taxed to render them perfect in every respect."

Of the boats mentioned above, the *Wm. Starkey* was named for one of the founders of the Boston Marine Society. A record of April 19, 1858 shows the following pilots attached to her: Captains P. H. Chandler, A. T. Hayden, R. S. Hunt, A. H. Josselyn, A. Nash and William Read.

The *Phantom* was mentioned in the 1843 memoirs of Erastus B. Badger, prominent Boston business man, in these words: "I was now approaching the age when I should learn a trade. Being very fond of the water, I was happy at a chance to go as an apprentice aboard the pilot boat *Phantom* to learn the piloting business in Boston Harbor and vicinity.

PILOT BOATS, IN BOSTON HARBOR.

1859

The articles were made out but not signed. My father changed his mind."

During the great snowstorm of January 18, 1857 when Boston Harbor was frozen solid, "as far down as the Castle," the *Phantom* was dragged ashore on the south side of George's Island but got off without injury. She was sold later to owners in Norfolk, Virginia.

It was on the *Phantom* that Warren Simpson entered the pilot service as an apprentice in 1846, under Captain J. K. Lunt. He served for four years, then succumbed to the California gold rush fever and shipped as a seaman on a square-rigger — the *Mary Merrill* — bound around Cape Horn. He arrived in San Francisco after a voyage of nine months during which much rough weather was encountered. Before going into the mining area he worked for a time on the pilot boat *Dancing Feather* from Boston, under Captain James L. Fowler who, with his son Franklin, had gone to California several months before Simpson got there. Later, Captain Fowler sent to Boston for a diver named Smith with whom he, his son and another man proceeded to the coast of Mexico where they searched the wreck of a ship which had sunk there with a load of treasure aboard. Simpson reported that this treasure hunt was successful and that Captain Fowler's share amounted to $100,000. In 1855 news of the discovery of gold in New South Wales lured Simpson to Australia but after an absence of eleven years he decided to return home to Boston. Here he became well known as the cabman with a stand for his horse and cab at the corner of Tremont and West Streets where for years he was a familiar figure in his long dark blue coat with a double row of brass buttons. Many of our older readers will undoubtedly remember him though they may not have known him by name. His interest in pilots and their work was maintained all through his long life.

The *Coquette,* one of the most admired of early American yachts, was described as low and graceful in the water, with

Photograph by Jos. G. Kennedy, Lake Stevens, Wash.   Courtesy of Ross W. Winde, Everett, Wash.

THE *COQUETTE*, YACHT AND PILOT BOAT

a clipper bow, resembling the famous yacht "America" in shape. She was designed by Lewis Winde, who was well on the way to establishing an outstanding record in planning small vessels and, later, pilot boats. In 1839 he was responsible for the design of the *Northern Light* whose sailing qualities had been admired by James A. Perkins, a prominent young Bostonian of liberal means and sporting instincts. As a result, Winde received an order for the designing and construction of the *Coquette* which was named for a bark of 420 tons built in 1844 at East Boston by Samuel Hall for the Perkins family. Winde was in partnership with Henry R. Clinkard, a shipwright, operating under the name of Winde & Clinkard. This proved to be a highly successful combination of talents. Their light work was done in Boston and the heavier vessels were built at their yard in Chelsea where the *Coquette* was laid down in the fall of 1845 and launched in the spring of 1846.

Mr. Perkins had been invited to bring the *Coquette* to New York and set out in a piping "norther," making a record run of the 284 miles between the two cities in 32 hours, averaging 9 knots an hour. She was entered in the second annual regatta of the New York Yacht Club and, according to contemporary reports "her model, and indeed her entire appearance excited the greatest admiration." Her first race was sailed in light weather and we're sorry to record that a small sloop won. However, on the run to Newport, R.I. which followed, the *Coquette* and the *Northern Light,* both Winde-designed, carried off the honors among the schooners of which the Club fleet was chiefly composed. During this cruise Mr. Perkins issued a challenge for the *Coquette* to sail any vessel in the New York Yacht Club for $500 a side. This was accepted by Commodore John C. Stevens (mentioned in our story on the *Sylph*) for his *Maria* and the race was set for October 10. The start was made in a heavy "northeaster" with the wind at better than 25 knots an hour and resulted

in victory for the *Coquette,* whereupon the Boston men glee-
fully hoisted a broom to the mainmast of the winner.

The racing skipper of the *Coquette* was Captain Elbridge
Gerry Martin, a Boston pilot, and when in 1849 Mr. Perkins
decided to sell the yacht it is said Captain Martin and a fellow
pilot, Captain Samuel Colby, obtained her at a very favorable
price. She was converted for pilot service, being in operation
for eighteen years until she was sold in 1867 to be used in
foreign trade. An interesting sidelight is that while she was
a pilot boat the *Coquette* was equipped with spars obtained
from David Sears of Boston from whom the Sears Building
derives its name.

The picture we have reproduced has an interesting story
of its own. Painted by C. Drew, an artist of some reputation
in his time, it was spotted by Lewis Winde in the ship
chandlery store of Charles Stearns on Commercial Street,
Boston. It was soiled and smoke-begrimed but Winde recognized it as the *Coquette,* had it cleaned and found it was a
faithful and spirited representation of the most famous vessel
he had designed. It was left to his son Henry. That was all
the information we had when we tried to locate this painting
for presentation in our brochure. Current directories revealed
no Henry Winde but in the telephone book there were two
Windes listed — Ronald H. and a Ronald H., Jr. A hopeful
call was made to the former and to our delight he was well
acquainted with the painting of the *Coquette,* which quite
naturally has become a cherished family heirloom. However,
we were told that the painting was about 3000 miles away —
in Everett, Washington — in the possession of an older cousin,
Ross W. Winde, to whom it had gone by inheritance. By use
of air mail, one of the many marvelous innovations which have
become commonplace since the days of the *Coquette,* we met
with cordial co-operation from the present owner who had a
color photo taken and sent to us for use here, for the interest
and pleasure of our readers.

Commonwealth of Massachusetts.

To *James M. Dolliver* of *Boston*

in the County of *Suffolk* **Greeting :**

Whereas, By Law, the Commissioners of Pilots for the State of Massachusetts, are empowered to appoint and commission Pilots in conformity with the Laws of the State :—Therefore, reposing especial trust and confidence in your ability, skill, and integrity, We, the undersigned, Commissioners of Pilots, for the State of Massachusetts, do, by these Presents, appoint you, the said

James M. Dolliver

to be a Pilot, for the Pilotage of Vessels

into and out of the Harbor or Port of *Boston*
Until this Commission shall be revoked or suspended,
by order of the Commissioners

You are, therefore, carefully and diligently to discharge the duties of a Pilot, for the Harbor of

Boston

aforesaid, and to take charge of any Vessel or Vessels, (except Fishing Vessels, and Vessels bound to or coming from any Port within the Commonwealth, and all Vessels of less than two hundred tons, sailing under a Coasting License.) You are to exhibit this Commission to the Master or Owner of any Vessel who may wish to see your authority to act as Pilot ; and you are to be governed by such rules and regulations, and to receive such fees, as are or may be prescribed, in conformity to the provisions of the Law.

Given at *Boston* Under the hands of the Commissioners of Pilots in and for the State of Massachusetts, this *Third* day of *October* A. D. *1855.*

Caleb Curtis
Solomon Freeman } **Commissioners.**
Geo. H. Devereux

N. B. You are directed to collect Six per cent. additional, on the amount of the rated fees, from the first day of July last, according to law.

Full Branch.

--◦◦{ 39 }◦◦--

CAPTAINS DOLLIVER AND CHANDLER, *PILOTS*

On February 2, 1859, and we all know how cold and windy it can be here in New England at that time of year, the British schooner *Caroline of Dartmouth* struck on rocks in approaching Boston and was abandoned by her crew. The Captain, James B. Apter of Brixham, refused to quit the ship, thinking it possible she might yet be saved. The next morning, when the pilot boat *Friend* approached, Apter was discovered lashed to the side of the *Caroline* in imminent danger of perishing from exposure to the severity of the weather. Captains James M. Dolliver and P. H. Chandler took off in a "canoe," as the "yawls" were then called, and succeeded in negotiating the perilous sea and saving Captain Apter who was exhausted and nearly frozen to death.

A graphic description of his plight was given in the report made by Apter to the authorities: "The efforts made for my salvation were of the most dangerous yet humane nature inasmuch as their course from the Pilot Boat to the vessel was in broken water nearly the whole way—and when I was lashed to the weather side of the vessel—seeing them manage their little boat with such skill as every seaman must admire—I was expecting every sea would fill their boat and dash them against the rocks—and was very much concerned for their safety, as they afterwards told me they were for mine—expecting I should be frozen to death, I being in that situation twenty-one hours—when I was taken from the wreck."

The British Government awarded to each of the pilots a gold medal bearing a portrait of Queen Victoria for their gallantry and humanity. Medals were also presented to Thomas Russell, Justice of the Police Court of Boston at that time, and Mrs. Russell who accompanied the two pilots on the *Friend* and, to quote from the official correspondence, ". . . They not only gave striking proof of their courage and humanity by going in the pilot boat, but by their encouragement and sympathy afforded material aid to the Pilots in the performance of their dangerous and gallant service."

The two pilots were also awarded silver medals by the Humane Society of Massachusetts for their uncommon courage and perseverance in saving Captain Apter's life.

By coincidence, as this is being written, the town of Brixham, home of Captain Apter, has been in the news in stories about the construction there of a reproduction of the *Mayflower*, the small craft which has such an outstanding place in the history of our nation. William A. Baker of Hingham, Mass., naval architect with the Bethlehem Steel Company, produced the working plans based on his studies of ships of the 17th century and information contained in Bradford's journals. This 20th century *Mayflower* is being built by the people of Great Britain as a good will gift to the people of the United States. It will become a featured part of the growing historical Pilgrim shrine being developed by the "Plimoth Plantation" at Plymouth, Massachusetts.

Brixham, in Devon, is located in the same county as Plymouth, England, and wooden ships have been built there for generations. Because of this background, it was not difficult to obtain experienced shipwrights who could do the hand labor required in producing a worthy reproduction. Much of the work is done with the adze and has to be executed with painstaking care which prolongs the job but it is expected that the finished vessel will sail across to our Plymouth next summer. Applications for the crossing have been received from all over the world despite the fact that the trip will be long and probably tough. All on board are to wear homespun such as the Pilgrims wore and passengers will have to sleep on deck as there will be no cabins for their accommodation. The only concession to our century will be a radio and rubber life rafts, which the British Ministry of Transport insists upon, and a camera to be used by the official photographer for recording the voyage.

CAPTAIN WILLIAM CARLTON FOWLER, PILOT

Born in Wiscasset, Maine, Captain Fowler went to sea at the age of 11 in a coasting vessel and later spent several years along the bleak coast of Labrador. He then headed southward to more comfortable climes and cruised on vessels in the Spanish Main and on voyages to South America and Liverpool. At one time he accumulated enough funds to become part owner of the schooner *Sea Flower* with which he engaged in the coastal trade, as master of the vessel. In 1833 he joined the pilot service on the *Favorite* under Captain Benjamin Swett. (At that time there were no numbers on sails of pilot boats.) In the summer of 1835 he took charge of the yacht *Sylph,* as mentioned in our chapter on that early yacht. He received his commission as a pilot later in 1835 from Governor Levi Lincoln and served his calling well and faithfully for over 50 years. During this period he was attached at various times to the *Boston,* the *Spy,* the *Sylph* when she became a pilot boat, the *Eben D. Jordan* and the *Hesper.* He and several other pilots financed the building of the *Relief* on which he served for several years until she was sold to the pilots of Mobile. His favorite boat, of which he was the owner, was the *Florence #6,* named for his wife. When he was on the *Hesper* he was the oldest pilot in active service while the owner, Captain George W. Lawler, was the youngest.

At the time of the famous episode during the "big freeze" of Boston Harbor in February 1844 when the *Britannia* was frozen in, it was Captain Fowler who laid out the course for the workmen to take in cutting a channel through the ice, and he also conducted her out to freedom. Some of the newspapers of the day gave credit to another for directing the release of the *Britannia* which was described as a feat of Herculean proportions, but later gave credit where it was due — to Captain Fowler.

One of the Captain's most satisfying activities during a long life was the establishment of the Boston Pilots' Relief Society in 1876 through his personal efforts.

Mrs. Florence Evans Bushee of Newburyport kindly loaned us a family scrapbook which provided most of the above information. We are also indebted to her for the use of the picture of the *Florence* reproduced below.

Courtesy of Mrs. Florence Evans Bushee

PILOT BOAT *FLORENCE*

This pilot boat of a little under 50 tons register was built at Boston in 1867 for Captain William Carlton Fowler, grandfather of Mrs. Bushee. The *Florence* had a long career in the pilotage service during which many famous pilots of Boston served on her.

CAPTAIN FRANKLIN FOWLER, PILOT

Franklin Fowler, mentioned in our story on the Pilot Boat Fleet of 1859, became a pilot when he returned to Boston, serving for twenty-five years on the *Hesper, Minerva, Florence* and *Liberty,* among other pilot boats. He was awarded a bronze medal by the Humane Society of Massachusetts while serving on the *Hesper* for his part in the rescue of members of the crew of the *Hattie L. Curtis* on September 26, 1888. Before his death in 1902 at the age of 60 he left directions for cremation, the ashes to be taken in charge by one of his oldest and dearest friends, also a pilot, and scattered on the waters of Massachusetts Bay. He also left a letter with careful directions as to the funeral services, one request being: "I desire to have the Rev. E. A. Horton cast off my lines." The Reverend Mr. Horton complied with his request in a very interesting and appropriate manner by composing the following verses which he read at the services:

> "Cast off the lines!" Our friend goes forth
> To voyage upon an unknown sea;
> His smiling face turns back to us
> And still his cheerful voice sings free.

> "Cast off the lines!" no fear, no doubt,
> For God is pilot on that sea.
> O Thou, who rulest time and tide,
> We trust his future course to Thee.

> "Cast off the lines!" Good-by! Good-by!
> With wistful looks we search the sea;
> Lo! love and mem'ry call him back—
> In loyal hearts his home shall be.

CAPTAIN GEORGE W. LAWLER, *PILOT*

Captain George W. Lawler was connected with the Boston pilot service for more than forty years. At the age of eleven he had sailed around the world in the *Ocean Belle* which was under command of a friend of the family. Young Lawler developed such a love for the sea on this voyage that he applied for employment in the pilot service through his brother-in-law Charles Hayden who was at that time agent for the pilots of Boston. He began his apprenticeship at the age of fifteen and when just out of his teens received his full Branch Pilot commission.

His first pilot boat was the *Lillie,* named for his mother, which was designed by the prominent naval architect Dennison J. Lawlor of Chelsea who was responsible for the design of many other fine pilot boats and yachts during the 1860's and 1870's. A Boston pilot boat was named for him in 1882 as related in the following chapter.

The *Lillie* was described as one of the most graceful of outline on the water and she was as sturdy as she was attractive in appearance. Captain Lawler's log, written when he was not quite twenty-one, tells how the *Lillie* weathered the terrific gale of January 25, 1879. In addition to the violence of the wind and the turbulent sea, snow and ice made conditions extremely hazardous. Ropes were frozen into the blocks, sails were frozen to the masts and anchors and chains were buried under ice, while the "yawls," or "canoes," which were bottoms up on deck were solidly frozen and immovable. Several of the men suffered severely from frostbite. Captain Lawler had heard that kerosene was helpful in such cases and tried it out. He saturated a woolen cloth in kerosene and held it against the frozen faces and hands and as if by magic the frost disappeared. This treatment has proved of great advantage to the pilots in succeeding years.

Courtesy of George S. Lawler, son of George W. Lawler

SILVER MEDAL AWARDED CAPTAIN LAWLER BY THE HUMANE SOCIETY OF MASSACHUSETTS

After 1849 it was the custom of the Humane Society to present their new Silver Medal, as the equivalent of the Gold Medal of former times, when the rescuer showed uncommon courage and perseverance in saving human life at the risk of his own.

PILOT BOAT *LILLIE*

After being caught out in Boston Bay, by the gale (velocity, 68 miles per hour), Saturday night, January 25, 1879.

Fortunately the *Lillie,* though crippled, survived her great ordeal and was towed by a tug boat to Gallups Island Wharf and later was taken by the police steamer *Protector* to her home wharf in Boston.

Dennison Lawlor's masterpiece pilot boat design was generally considered to be the *Hesper,* 93.99 tons, the largest in the fleet at the time, which he also designed for Captain George Lawler. Built by Howard & Montgomery of Chelsea, she aroused much favorable comment at New York when Captain Lawler sailed her over there, with some friends aboard, to watch the *Puritan* and *Genesta* race in 1885.

In April of 1886 there was a strike on in the Boston fishing fleet and Thomas F. McManus, a well-known fish merchant of the city who had a great interest in boat racing and was a boat designer of no mean reputation, felt that the time was ripe for testing the racing prowess of the fishing vessels. He went to Commodore J. Malcolm Forbes to obtain his backing of the idea. Commodore Forbes promptly offered a donation of $100 for a race to be open to all two-masted working vessels. As McManus was on his way to the door Forbes called him back and said he would also give a cup, in addition to the money, if the *Hesper* was added to the racing group. If she won, she would get the cup and if a fishing boat came in first the winner would get both the cup and the money.

Other leading Boston citizens and businessmen including General Charles J. Paine, Nathaniel Thayer, E. V. R. Thayer,

Courtesy of the Pilots of Boston
Pilot Boat *HESPER*
Winner of first Fishermen's Race in which she was entered by special request, as related in the text.

J. Montgomery Sears, Commodore H. S. Hovey, Charles A. Longfellow and George Ripley Howe added to the fund which, before race day on Saturday, May 1, amounted to well over $1,500.

Eleven fishing schooners took part in what is said to have been the first fishermen's race, news of which had aroused great interest in the city. There was some opposition to the entry of the *Hesper* but when the terms of the awarding of first prize were explained the objections subsided. The course was from an imaginary line between the judges' steamer and a buoy in range with Boston Light down to a buoy off Minot's Light, Cohasset, to Davis Ledge and thence to Half Way Rock off the Beverly Shore, then back to the starting point. The *Hesper*, with Commodore Forbes aboard as a guest, won the spirited contest and the prize cup. The fishing schooner *John H. McManus*, skippered by Captain John O'Brien, crossed the finish line forty minutes later, thereby winning $1500. in prize money. As a result of his active promotion of this event, Mr. McManus came to be known as "The father of Fishermen's Races."

The skillful Captain Lawler, described as a handsome, lovable man with brown side whiskers, rosy cheeks and a cheery smile, figured in several rescues during his long career as a pilot. In recognition of his courage in saving the lives of the crew of the schooner *William D. Cargill* which was wrecked in a heavy snowstorm in the lower harbor in 1884, he was awarded a silver medal by the Massachusetts Humane Society, shown in the accompanying illustration. He was awarded a bronze medal by the same Society for rescuing four survivors of the schooner *Hattie L. Curtis*, 1888.

William M. McMilan, later a pilot but then Boatkeeper on the *Hesper*, received a Silver medal from the Humane Society "for rescuing from a raft at sea, in a small canoe, at great personal peril, the crew of the schooner 'Hattie L. Curtis'—26th September, 1888."

Pilot Boat *D. J. LAWLOR*

Pilot Boat *D. J. LAWLOR*

The original of the picture on the opposite page is rather unusual as the hull is of velvet and the sails are of silk. It was presented to our Bank by Captain Nathaniel W. Abbott, a former Boston pilot now retired. It may be seen in the collection at our State Street Office, in the Trust Department.

The *Lawlor* was built in 1882 by Porter Keene at Weymouth, Mass., and was considered the best heavy weather boat in the service. She was named for Dennison J. Lawlor, the famous pilot boat designer.

During a violent "northwester" early in the morning of January 5, 1895, in a dense fog, the *Lawlor* was rammed and sunk by the fishing schooner *Horace B. Parker* of Gloucester, Captain Thomas, about two miles off Minot's Light, Cohasset. Having been "manned out," the *Lawlor* was returning to port in charge of #1 Boatman Albert Laurine with three other apprentices and the cook, Rudolph Harrison, when the accident occurred. Harrison jumped from the bowsprit of the *Lawlor* to the deck of the fisherman. When Laurine tried to follow the bowsprit broke and he fell into the raging sea. The crew of the *Parker* did all in their power to save him and the three others on the *Lawlor* but all the lifesaving apparatus, ropes and lifeboats were covered with a foot of ice and could not be used.

The *Lawlor* was owned in part by Captain William V. Abbott and his associate Pilot Captains John Leary, William W. McPhee and William Fairfield, all of whom providentially escaped the disaster as they had been put aboard inbound vessels to pilot them into Boston.

PILOT BOAT *LOUISE*

The water color reproduced above was presented to our Bank by Captain Nathaniel W. Abbott, a former pilot of Boston Harbor, now retired. It may be seen in the collection at our State Street Office, in the Trust Department.

The Pilot Boat *LOUISE*

The *Louise* has the distinction of being commemorated in verse because of an exciting episode which occurred one rough, snowy autumn day of 1900 just after her "yawl" had put Pilot John C. Fawcett aboard the R.M.S. *Saxonia*.

On its way back to the *Louise* the "yawl" overturned. Though the two boatmen succeeded in righting it, the water it had taken on caused it to capsize again. Fortunately both men managed to get hold of the "yawl" and held on until they drifted toward the *Saxonia*. Ladders were lowered over the side of the liner and her First Mate climbed down with a lifebuoy which he tossed to the men, thereby unquestionably saving their lives. The "yawl" disappeared beneath the *Saxonia* and was never seen again.

In trying to maneuver in the rough weather to rescue her boatmen, the *Louise* split her main boom and was so badly damaged that she was rendered incapable of being of assistance. Thinking the boatmen were lost, her flag was put at half-mast.

One of the men saved was Eric, brother of the late pilot Capt. Frederick W. Ahlquist who told us about this occurrence. He was on shore when the *Louise* made her way into port and, seeing the position of the flag, he remarked to her Captain: "I suppose I know who one of them is," meaning his brother. The reply was a sad "Yes." Naturally Captain Ahlquist had a very gloomy time until some hours later he was told that his brother had been saved and was probably up in Boston celebrating his narrow escape. The passengers of the *Saxonia* had taken up a collection for the two men who were rescued so they had the funds with which to celebrate if they so desired.

A spontaneous piece of poetry describing this event in detail was written by M. Holdsworth, a passenger on the *Saxonia*. It is too long for us to present more than a few lines here but we think they will give a good idea as to the nature of the rest of the poem. After recounting how the pilot was put aboard the *Saxonia* in spite of the tempest, the poet comes to the capsizing of the "yawl:"

> . . . There, in the midst of the seething main,
> They struggled and fought to reach again
> That storm-tossed bark on the angry seas,
> Their haven of rest, "The Pilot Louise;"
> And when, for a time, they were lost to our view,
> We fondly imagined them safe with the crew;
> But oh, how different from what we surmised,
> For see — there she is; — O God — and capsized!
> And there, on the mighty waters afloat,
> Clinging like death to each end of the boat,
> Were the two gallant lads of "The Pilot Louise,"
> And the sight made our very heart's blood freeze.
> Can nothing be done to save those souls
> That cling to the boat as she tosses and rolls?

> Then over the side our First Mate goes,
> And round the brave lads a lifebuoy throws;
> And then, when at last they are safely aboard,
> Not a soul on the ship but said "Thank the Lord."

The *Louise,* among other notable craft, was designed and built at East Boston by Ambrose A. Martin whose father and son were pilots. She replaced the *Columbia* which was wrecked on Scituate beach during the great "Portland" storm of November 1898. Three of the pilots who started out with the *Columbia* when she made her last sail from Boston, Captains John and Joseph Fawcett and William V. Abbott, were co-owners of the *Louise* with Captains Watson Dolliver and Bruce McLean. She had a very successful launching in the presence of nearly 1000 spectators who had gathered in Martin's big shipyard at Jeffries Point and on the adjacent wharves. Pretty, young, eleven-year-old Louise Fawcett, daughter of Captain John and niece of Captain Joseph, christened what was termed by the contemporary press "the new and magnificent pilot boat *Louise.*"

BOSTON PILOT BOATS AT SHANGHAI

Through the friendliness of the late Horace Allen Arnold, a licensed pilot of Shanghai, whose exotic address in 1938 when we first heard from him was 26 The Bund, Shanghai, China, we have a copy of "The Log of the Shanghai Pilot Service, 1831–1932," by Pilot Captain George Philip who received his commission as a pilot there in 1918. Captain Arnold remained in the pilot service at Shanghai until driven out by Japanese bombers during World War II. He returned to Amityville, New York, where he made his home until his death in September, 1949.

The "Log" covers the period from the arrival at that port of the first foreign trading vessel to the retirement of the author. This first vessel, the East India Company's *Lord Amherst,* was unsuccessful in efforts to obtain a pilot and it was not until some years later that pilots, other than Chinese, could be engaged. These natives had a very good knowledge of the waters of the mouth of the Yangtze Kiang river and along the adjacent coast and islands, but most of them were in league with pirates and lost no opportunity for putting vessels ashore where they were subsequently looted. By 1844 several foreign pilots were available for service but the first one of record was listed in 1847. From then on the history of pilotage in that Chinese port over the period recorded by Captain Philip parallels in general that of Boston. However, in addition to natural hazards, the pilots of Shanghai had to be constantly on the alert in the early years to avoid the rapacity of pirates which resulted in death to some and narrow escapes for others. From 1867 to 1932 pilots of eleven nationalities held licenses at Shanghai. While there were 82 British pilots — more than those of any other nation, Americans were second with 33, which is one reason for including this material about Shanghai in our

Courtesy of Charles I. Lampee

PILOT BOAT *DANIEL WEBSTER*
Boston, San Francisco and Shanghai

brochure. There were several familiar Boston names among the Americans appearing on the Shanghai roster. Though we could not trace them to our city, it is reasonable to assume that some of them were from here as this was during the exciting and enterprising era when Boston ships and Boston men were known in every port of the Seven Seas.

At least three pilot boats, the *Daniel Webster,* the *Golden Gate* and the *Syren* had Boston backgrounds. The *Daniel Webster* was built at Chelsea, Mass. in 1851. In 1853 she left for San Francisco whence she sailed for Shanghai, China, in 1865 to become a member of the pilot fleet there in 1866. The *Golden Gate* was Boston-owned and when she arrived in Shanghai in 1865 was the largest pilot schooner operating there. The *Syren* was purchased for himself and others for service in China by Robert Bennet Forbes, grandfather of Allan Forbes. She reached Shanghai in 1866 and soon was entered in a race with the *Golden Gate* and the *Geo. F. Seaward,* also foreign-owned. Large amounts were wagered and we are sorry we cannot report a victory for either of the erstwhile Boston boats, as the *Geo. F. Seaward* was the winner. In 1870, in addition to these three pilot boats there were ten others in service at Shanghai which were listed as foreign-owned. Incidentally, there was also a tug, *Bunker Hill,* operating in Shanghai from 1863 to 1874, and possibly longer.

The *Daniel Webster* operated until 1892 when she was driven ashore with three pilots aboard. All were rescued but the boat was lost.

The oil painting of the *Daniel Webster* reproduced here is owned by Mr. Charles I. Lampee of Winchester, Mass., whose two grandfathers served on the *Daniel Webster* in the Boston pilotage service—Captain William R. Lampee as a pilot and Thomas Cooper as an apprentice. (He later won his commission as a pilot.)

When the great man for whom she was named died on October 24, 1852, the pilots of the *Daniel Webster* wanted to attend the funeral which was to be held from his Marshfield home. They sailed down there on the day of the funeral but, unfortunately, there was a flat calm and the pilot boat was so far out that it was not possible to row ashore in time to attend the services, much to their regret.

The *Golden Gate* was lost in a typhoon in 1871 and the *Syren* was run down and sunk by a steamer in 1896. All but one of those aboard the *Syren* got away safely. Yankee pilot schooners, or schooners built after that style, were said to be far superior to others in the Shanghai service.

The custom at Shanghai was for all arrangements for the examination of an apprentice to be given by the pilot to whom he had been indentured. The pilot had to certify that the apprentice had carried out his duties faithfully, had obeyed all his orders as well as the pilotage regulations of the Port, and was fully qualified to fulfill the duties of a licensed pilot. Apparently one pilot, whose name is not revealed, heeded the urgings of his heart instead of his head in recommending an apprentice for examination as the record reads:

> Apprentice Pilot, Mr. H. P. Ellis failed in his examination for a second time. The Board found him lacking in local knowledge and extremely slow and hesitating in giving his answers in seamanship and the Rule of the Road and he, moreover, being now in his sixtieth year, and in general appearance and manner giving no promise that he would ever be able to perform efficiently the duties of a licensed pilot for the Port of Shanghai, the Board feels, in duty bound, to recommend him to seek other employment more suitable to his age and condition.

The Shanghai Licensed Pilots' Association was established in 1900 and resulted in much improved and more reliable service. This corresponds somewhat to the movement in Boston which culminated in 1901.

TWENTY-FOUR HOURS ON A PILOT BOAT

It was an August day when we were able to accept the invitation of the pilots to spend a day and night aboard their *Pilot #1*, then on station in the Bay.

Transportation down the harbor was provided by an old friend, George W. Bentley, in his speedy cruiser the *Yankee-D*, a name remindful of the Division (YD) in which we had both served overseas in World War I. We brought aboard, as a special guest, Leonard H. "Steamer" Nason, who had gained a fine reputation as the author of several popular books based on his experience in that same War. Incidentally, he served again in World War II with the rank of Colonel.

We boarded the pilot boat directly from the *Yankee-D* and during the next 24 hours saw firsthand the picking up of pilots from outgoing ships, the sending of pilots to board incoming craft, and made one trip into Nahant to pick up additional pilots for duty aboard our pilot boat. We also saw how the special pilot boat lights were shown to indicate that pilots were ready for service. Turning out of our bunks at 2 o'clock in the morning to watch Captain Richard A. Roach put aboard an incoming liner was an interesting experience. The "yawl" which took the pilots between the pilot boat and the larger craft also carried a light which added to the interest in watching it as it bobbed up and down on its trips to and from the *Pilot*. The lantern is a special box type about 9 inches square with a magnifying bull's-eye on each of three sides. Light is furnished by a "plumber's candle" about 1¼ inches in diameter and 5 inches high. Special matches are kept handy for use in lighting the candle in windy weather. The lantern is fixed to a stick and lodged in the after thwarts of the "yawl." Years ago, in addition to the light at the mast head, the pilot boat used a turpentine flare which was flashed at brief but frequent intervals to signal its location. Such a flare is still kept aboard but an electric blinker is used for signalling, flashing high so the light will show up well on the sails.

As our day wore on, we had a close-up view of the way a pilot is put aboard an incoming vessel when Captain Frederick L. Bailey was taken aboard a big passenger ship. While the pilots and apprentices are not uniformed, they certainly handle their duties with speed and precision which shows long practice and training. The "yawl," which weighs about 800 lbs., is towed behind the pilot boat in good weather, and as it is drawn up, the pilot steps aboard and the two boatmen follow. After being towed by the pilot boat under the lee of the larger vessel, the "yawl" is set free and the men row toward the craft to be boarded. It is all done rapidly and, apparently, with the greatest of ease. After the pilot has "gone over the side" the pilot boat continues out ahead of the vessel and, keeping the "yawl" in sight at all times, turns in readiness to pick it up as soon as it leaves the ship. Soon the "yawl" is in tow again and the pilot boat resumes its leisurely patrol. The average boarding time, by the way, is between 6 and 10 minutes.

The last bit of indoctrination on our trip came the following morning when we were put off in the "yawl" to return to the *Yankee-D* which had come out to get us. We found then that the easy nonchalance with which a pilot steps from the deck of the pilot boat into the "yawl" is very deceptive and requires expert timing. In an effort to imitate the pilots' dexterity it soon became apparent to the tyro that there is quite a rise and fall on the part of the "yawl" and unless the transfer is made very carefully trouble is ahead. Fortunately, by using a cautious approach we negotiated the transfer and arrived safely on the *Yankee-D* after a most enjoyable and interesting sojourn aboard the *Pilot*.

PILOT BOATS IN THE "PORTLAND" STORM

When the pilots adopted their new form of organization in 1901, requiring five instead of eight boats, the *Varuna,* the *America,* the *Louise,* the *Liberty* and the *Adams* were continued in the service while the *Hesper,* the *Minerva* and the *Sylph* were sold. Captain James H. Reid of the America #1 piloted out the last vessel under the old system. Under the new system, Captain William McMilan was the first to take out a vessel — the *Montauk* — and Captain Watson S. Dolliver was the first to bring one in — the *Turconian.* During a long career in the piloting service, the most hazardous experience of the *Varuna* occurred the night of the "Portland" storm of November 26 and 27, 1898. When the storm broke she was about 20 miles off Minot's Light, Cohasset. Captain William H. Fairfield had himself lashed to the wheel and remained on duty 24 hours, not allowing himself to be relieved until two of his ribs were broken from beating against the binnacle. The foresail was carried away and ice and snow added to the difficulties encountered. However, the *Varuna* survived the terrible ordeal by following the instructions given by Captain Fairfield as he was carried drenched and injured to his bunk: "Keep her headed up, make a straight wake; she is made of oak and copper and can stand it." One of her two "yawls" was crushed and the other was damaged, her lee rail was carried away and the morning light revealed that her deck was completely covered with sand blown from sandbars when she was off Cape Cod during the night. Crippled as she was, she was still carrying on as a pilot boat should and, repairing her damaged "yawl" as well as possible, it was used to put a pilot aboard an incoming Philadelphia vessel which then towed the *Varuna* into port. When they arrived they were amazed to be greeted by every whistle in the harbor as they had been considered victims of the great storm because the lost rail, bearing her name, had been washed up on the shore of Cape Cod.

Courtesy of Charles M. Wright

PILOT BOAT *VARUNA*

Named for the Vedic king of the waters of early Hindu mythology, the *Varuna* was an 86-ton center-board schooner designed by Edward Burgess and built by Howard & Montgomery in 1890 at Chelsea, Massachusetts.

While the *Varuna* outlived the storm, the *Columbia* met with disaster. She was about 80 miles offshore and having been "manned out" when Captain William Abbott, the last pilot aboard, had been placed on the incoming steamer *Ohio*, the *Columbia* was headed toward Boston. It was generally believed that the terrific gale stripped her of her sails and that she tried to ride out the storm at anchor. Judging by the condition of her anchor chains it appeared that the waves were too powerful and broke the chains, setting her adrift. In her helpless condition she was driven solidly aground on the beach at Scituate off Cedar (or Lighthouse) Point, losing all five men aboard.

Courtesy of Charles M. Wright

PILOT BOAT *COLUMBIA*

Built of white oak at the East Boston yard of Ambrose A. Martin for Captain Thomas Cooper in 1894, she was destined to have a short career in the pilotage service of Boston. During the great "Portland" storm of November 26 and 27, 1898, she was driven ashore at Scituate with the loss of all five men aboard and had to be abandoned.

Too badly damaged for reconditioning, the *Columbia* remained on the beach at Sand Hills for over thirty years, being used at various times as a tea room, a summer home and as a museum of antiques and curiosities of the sea. At the same time she was a magnet for sightseers and also served as a breakwater. Otis Barker of Scituate owned her at one time and introduced many reminders of the "home on the sands" of Old Peggotty and Little Emily, widely known characters in "David Copperfield," one of the most familiar books by Charles Dickens. There is a small display of pictures in the Trust Department at our State Street Office showing the *Columbia* before and after the wreck. An interesting sidelight about Scituate, which, by the way, has seen many wrecks down through the years, is that a small ship 83 feet long named *Columbia* was built there on the North River in 1773. This *Columbia* became famous as the first American vessel to circumnavigate the globe, going around Cape Horn to our Northwest coast where she discovered the great river in Oregon which commemorates her name. She traded hardware, tools, toys and beads for furs which were taken to China and traded for tea which was brought back to Boston. On her return after an absence of almost three years her arrival was greeted with artillery salutes and the officers and owners of the vessel were given a dinner by Governor Hancock.

The latest wreck on the shore of Scituate was that of the Italian freighter *Etrusco* which went aground during the great blizzard of March 16th this year, not far from where the *Columbia* struck in 1898. As many of our readers will recall, all thirty men aboard the *Etrusco* were rescued by the Coast Guard via breeches buoy early in the morning of March 17th, after a harrowing night spent on the unfortunate ship. Incidentally that blizzard and the severe one which followed on March 19th were rather rough for the pilots down the Bay.

United Press Photograph

ETRUSCO on the Beach at Scituate

WARTIME SERVICE

According to "A History of American Privateers" by Edgar S. Maclay (published in 1899) during the War of 1812 many of the first privateers to go to sea to "burn, sink and destroy" vessels of the enemy were small pilot boats, mounting one Long Tom amidship, with several smaller guns, and carrying crews of fifty to sixty men. The chief dependence of the men in battle was on muskets, cutlasses and boarding pikes.

As soon as it was known that War had been declared, a swift pilot boat hastened across the Atlantic to Gothenburg, Sweden, under orders to give warning to all American merchantmen then in the ports of Sweden, Denmark, Prussia and Russia. In this way a large number of our merchant craft were saved from capture.

During the Spanish-American War the pilots of Boston volunteered for service, as did their successors during World Wars I and II. The whole staff went under the jurisdiction of the Navy early in 1917. Guns and searchlights were mounted on the pilot boats and additional navy personnel served aboard these craft "for the duration." The *Liberty* and *Louise* were under command of Ensigns of the regular Navy and each was presented with a bronze plaque, the wording on which is given later. These plaques are preserved in the headquarters of the Pilots of Boston, as souvenirs of their service in World War I. All Navy pilotage was rendered free of charge and met with highest commendation. The boats were kept far outside Boston harbor, continually on patrol. All vessels approaching the entrance to the harbor had to report to the pilot boat to get the password of the day which had to be given to the warships on guard farther in, before they were permitted to proceed. Frequently in rough weather great difficulty arose in trying to signal the password from boat to ship. If a vessel failed to stop a shot soon brought her to attention.

--•⊰{ 65 }⊱•--

THE SECRETARY OF THE NAVY

WASHINGTON

14 November 1932

To all whom this may concern:

When the United States entered the World War the
American Pilots Association, with its branch state pilots
in the parts of the United States voluntarily placed their
Pilot Boats, equipment and service at the disposal of the
United States Navy, and performed efficient and valuable
service to their country.

In time of peace these Pilots meet all incoming vessels at the entrance of the harbors and guide them safely
into port. They maintain a highly efficient service which
is the development of many years of experience.

Conditions in the various ports vary and are constantly
changing, and in our opinion the present system maintained by
the Pilots is a valuable safeguard to the water-borne commerce
of our country.

Secretary, U. S. Navy

The Assistant Secretary, U.S.Navy

The original of this letter from the Hon. Charles Francis Adams, when
Secretary of the Navy, has an honored place in the headquarters of the
Pilots of Boston. It is of special interest to the bank as later Mr. Adams
was Chairman of the Board of the State Street Trust Company.

At the time of the German submarine foray off Cape Cod and George's Bank in July, 1918, several fishing schooners were sunk in the latter area. One of the pilot boats picked up a dory with ten men from one of the fishermen and landed them in Boston.

The wording on the plaques mentioned earlier was as follows:

U.S.S. Louise, No. 2
Section Patrol No. 1230
Was in the
United States Navy
during the War of 1917

This Vessel was patriotically placed at the Service
of the Government by her owners
Boston Pilots' Relief Society
Boston, Mass.

The plaque awarded the *Liberty* was the same, except that it bore her name and number (3). She was in Section Patrol No. 1229.

When World War II came along, the pilots again entered the service of our country, this time as temporary reserve officers of the U.S. Coast Guard, as shown in the illustration which accompanies this chapter. This was the first time that pilots, as a national group, were made an integral part of the military establishment. Wearing Coast Guard uniforms, they piloted troop transports, ships loaded with explosives, and many other naval vessels whose officers were not familiar with our port. These movements ran into the thousands and were accomplished without a single serious accident to ships or personnel. During this War the lighted buoys in the harbor were extinguished. Also, the pilots had to keep on the alert to beware of mines when the harbor was so protected. The two current pilot boats in service, the *Pilot* #1 and the *Roseway* #2, each proudly carries a plaque bearing the following inscription:

In Recognition of
The Valuable Service
Performed by
PILOT
during World War II
U.S. Coast Guard

The plaque on the *Roseway* bears her name, of course. The wartime designation of the *Pilot* was CG811 and that of the *Roseway*, CG812.

In the October, 1945, issue of the "Washington News Digest," in a fine article entitled "The Pilots of Our Ports," Congressman Frank W. Boykin of Alabama, long time member of the House Merchant Marine and Fisheries Committee, made the following statement: "For three years the pilots have carried a double load. In addition to the stormy seas and natural navigational hazards which prevail in peace time as well as in war, they were required to pilot the ships and convoys through complicated mine fields and the narrow openings of the anti-submarine nets guarding our seaboard ports. The size of the job can be told in a few figures. During 1944 the pilots handled 120,000 assignments without a single major casualty, and not one of these vessels, loaded with troops or war equipment, was delayed because of the unavailability of a pilot."

It may have been noticed by many of our readers that during World War II, at least, for security reasons the newspapers dropped the publication of ship arrivals and departures for the period from December 9, 1941 until May 29, 1945, on orders of the government.

Courtesy of the Boston Herald Traveler Corporation

PILOTS OF BOSTON TAKING THE OATH AS OFFICERS OF THE U. S. COAST GUARD (T.R.), DECEMBER 11, 1942, FOR SERVICE DURING WORLD WAR II.

Left to right: Clarence Fralic, Nathaniel W. Abbott, Paul B. Elder, Clarence A. Martin, Donald H. Weaver, Stanley R. Balcom, Frank W. Harriman, George R. Lauriat, Jr., David F. Bentham, Melvin R. Jackson, Llewellyn W. McMilan, Richard A. Roach, Patrick J. Sullivan, Alexander Holmes, Jr., Malcolm A. MacDonald, William H. Lewis, Burton H. Eddy and Lieutenant Commander William B. Corning, U. S. Coast Guard Reserve.

All full Branch Pilots over 35 years of age were commissioned Lieutenant Commanders. Of the above group, P. J. Sullivan was commissioned as a Lieutenant and Clarence Fralic was given the rank of Lieutenant, Junior Grade. Frederick C. Gevalt, the senior pilot, was sworn in prior to the induction pictured above, in recognition of his seniority. Later he was promoted to Commander.

The remaining pilots who were on duty in the Bay were commissioned at other times, as follows: I. C. Bailey, E. D. Child, H. R. Frye and G. W. Poor as Lieutenant Commanders, and W. H. Lewis, Jr., Lieutenant (J. G.). Clarence E. Doane, Agent for the Pilots, was given the rank of Lieutenant. During the period up to November 30, 1945, when they returned to civilian status, as older pilots retired the new ones were also sworn into Coast Guard Service. The apprentices were taken into the service as enlisted personnel.

Pilots of Boston Harbor

Name	Year Commissioned
FRANK W. HARRIMAN	1926
ALEXANDER HOLMES, JR.	1928
DAVID F. BENTHAM	1930
GEORGE W. POOR	1933
BURTON H. EDDY	1934
EDGAR D. CHILD	1935
GEORGE R. LAURIAT, JR.	1936
MELVIN R. JACKSON	1937
MALCOLM A. MACDONALD	1937
PATRICK J. SULLIVAN	1939
PAUL B. ELDER	1941
CLARENCE FRALIC	1942
JOHN P. CUSHMAN, JR.	1943
JAMES E. FRYE	1943
JOSEPH I. CORDES, JR.	1945
MELVIN F. LIVINGSTONE	1947
C. SHELTON COLLINS	1950
WILLIAM G. JENKINS	1951
LEWIS S. DOANE	1952
IRVING H. GARDNER	1952
CHARLES F. CROCKER, JR.	1953
JAMES B. CHAMBERS, JR.	1954
JUSTUS A. BAILEY	1955
ROBERT E. DERMODY	1955

PILOT HEADQUARTERS

One of the "Rules and Regulations" issued by the Pilot Commissioners for District One, Port of Boston, under the heading "Location of Pilot Office," reads as follows:

> *The Pilots of the Port of Boston shall keep an office in a central location on or near the water front, where all communications may be left for them, and it shall be the duty of the Pilots, when in Boston, to call at said office twice a day at least.*

Mr. James E. Bagley, Jr., Treasurer of the Proprietors of Boston Pier, or the Long Wharf, present landlords of the pilots, reported that the earliest records he could find showed that the pilots were tenants at Lewis Wharf on October 2, 1880 and may have been there prior to that date. They remained there until August 29, 1925 when they were burned out late one night, losing most of their early records, thus adding to the difficulties of obtaining much information which would have been very helpful in the preparation of this brochure.

Fortunately, Mr. Charles I. Lampee of Winchester, Mass. whose two grandfathers were pilots, made available to us a Boston Sunday "Post" of April 17, 1904, which contains a good description of the pilot quarters on Lewis Wharf and the "Post" granted us permission to use excerpts from the article mentioned. There were two rooms—the smaller one for washing up, changing clothes or taking a nap between calls, and a large one where the pilots on the "shore watch" gathered while waiting for notice to take a ship out of the harbor. In those days most of the older pilots wore beards so they made quite a picturesque group as they relaxed in their easy chairs. The walls of the room were covered with sea pictures, drawings of notable sea captains and pictures of early pilot boats, while

Whereas

The Boston Pilots

since its inception has been devoted to the continuing development of all phases of the great Port of Boston; and

Whereas over the years the members of the Boston Pilots have been unselfish and untiring in their efforts to promote the Port of Boston; and

Whereas the Boston Pilots has always been generous in the expenditure of both time and money in the interest of the Port of Boston and in cooperation with the Port of Boston Commission.

Now therefore be it Resolved that on this 9th day of September in the year of Our Lord one thousand nine hundred and fifty-five, we the members of the Port of Boston Commission commend the Boston Pilots for its outstanding contribution to the welfare of the Port of Boston.

The Commonwealth of Massachusetts
by the Port of Boston Commission

William H. Gulliver
J. Douglas Lawson
John T. Long
Richard J. Goodnich
James J. Healy

SCROLL PRESENTED TO THE

BOSTON PILOTS ON SEPTEMBER 9, 1955

BY THE PORT OF BOSTON COMMISSION

marine glasses, charts and compasses filled the window sills and shelves. At that time there were 34 pilots who were divided into two watches. Seventeen went down the harbor each Monday morning to board the four pilot boats then in service. One cruised off Highland Light, another off Cape Ann, while the other two patrolled around Boston Light and the Lightship. The pilots were ashore one week and at sea the next. After they had brought in ships, those on duty in the Bay took the first available outgoing craft to be picked up by the "canoe" from the pilot boat to which they were attached.

The present pilot headquarters are also adorned with many photographs and some paintings of former pilot boats and piloting scenes, as well as plaques awarded for war service and other tributes but, of course, they are of more modern vintage than those mentioned as being in the 1904 quarters.

After the fire, the pilots occupied temporarily part of the Wharf office at 67 Commercial Wharf, moving on October 1st, 1925, to 74 Long Wharf. When this space was needed by the United Fruit Company, tenants of most of the shed space at Long Wharf, for expansion of its banana business, the pilots moved on December 31, 1932 to the Harbor Building (now the Sheraton Building) on Atlantic Avenue where they remained until January 1, 1934 when they moved to their present quarters on the fourth floor at 69 Long Wharf. From here they get an excellent view of the harbor where the tug boats ply back and forth like giant water bugs, the gulls cruise overhead, planes approaching or leaving Logan International Airport fly even higher and small fishing boats with their bright sails give color to the scene. The building where they are located is said to be the first granite block built in Boston and was erected in 1845 for the U.S. Government as a bonded warehouse. The name "Custom House Block" stands out in bold granite letters high up on the face of the building.

Mr. Bagley is also active in the management of Commercial Wharf and Lewis Wharf so he was in a strategic position to give

Photograph by George M. Cushing, Jr.   *Courtesy of the Pilots of Boston*

Record of Incoming and Outgoing Vessels

The photograph reproduced above was taken on February 3, 1956 in the headquarters of the Pilots of the Port of Boston. The blackboard shows, in the left-hand column, the vessels expected inbound, while the section on the right lists those outbound. At the left of the blackboard are the names of the pilots in the order of their going on duty. When the pilot at the top goes out, the white board bearing his name is put at the bottom of the list and in due course gets to the top again. The seven names at the bottom indicate those who were out "in the Bay" at the time the photograph was taken. When a pilot is taken off the craft he is piloting outbound and reports aboard the pilot boat in the Bay, he takes his turn in rotation in bringing in vessels. Thus this "endless chain" procedure is carried out both ashore and afloat.

There is another blackboard in the headquarters listing vessels on which dates of movement have not been set.

The room where these boards are kept might be compared to what flying pilots call their "ready room."

When you see in your newspapers the record of daily arrivals and sailings of ships in Boston Harbor, you can rejoice or sympathize with the pilots, depending on the weather report of the day, as practically all vessels on the list are guided in and out of the harbor, in fair weather or foul, by that group of men sometimes referred to as "The Greeters of the Port."

us this information on the various offices of the pilots.

Many modern office buildings have signs in their lobbies reading "Peddlers and Beggars not Allowed" but when we began work on this publication we discovered that the pilots had a much better deterrent to such visitors than any sign could be. There are 45 steps up to their fourth-floor base of operations and those are in a straightaway steep flight from bottom to top,—no graceful curves, nothing but stairs—a rather discouraging sight!

In the old days, before the invention of the electric telegraph, word of the approach of vessels was signalled from hilltop to hilltop by "visual telegraph," thus accounting for the many "Telegraph Hills" along our coast from Martha's Vineyard to Boston. At one time there were thirteen of these signal stations between West Chop and Dorchester Heights. The Old State House at the head of State Street was once used as a station for the benefit of merchants and ship owners of our city so they would get advance notice of the arrival of vessels in which they had special interest.

Nowadays the pilot office and their two pilot boats are equipped with VHF radio-telephones enabling them to maintain instant communication concerning sailings and arrivals. This information is transmitted from pilot headquarters to the steamship companies and agents, terminal operators and other interested groups. Through use of this modern device, the number of pilots needed aboard the boat in the Bay is known in advance and they avoid having it "manned out," that is, the condition when all pilots on a boat have been put aboard incoming vessels. Thus there are always pilots on the boat available for service and replacements can be made as more "good" ships come in, the term the pilots use for those requiring guidance into the harbor.

The location of present pilot headquarters has a long and interesting history. Built in 1710, Long Wharf formed an extension of King Street (now State) some 2000 feet into the

UNITED STATES LINES

UNITED STATES LINES COMPANY

PIER 60, NORTH RIVER, NEW YORK 11, N.Y.

PANAMA PACIFIC LINE
AMERICAN PIONEER LINE

S.S.American Scout,
Boston, Massachusetts,
November 6th.1955.

Boston Pilots,
69 Long Wharf,
Boston, Mass.

Gentlemen:
      Our ship, "American Scout", United States Lines,
took pilot off the Boston Lightship,early in the morning
of Saturday,November 5th. Weather was foul,a Northeast gale
was on and a heavy sea running.Three ships embarked pilots
before us and all hands had a lively time,in fact it was a
"glowing hour" for all concerned.
      I shall not discuss the merits or the drawbacks
of your facilities as opposed to,say a powered launch.Rather
than criticize I wish to express my admiration and wonder
at what I saw that morning.
      The schooner was handled with nerve and skill and
the people in the dinghy elicited our admiration.You all gave
yourselves to the job in hand,fired with the traditional pride
that "the station must be manned." You did this, knowing that
at any moment your wives could be widowed!
      I was grateful to see big Captain Eddy "hit that
ladder". When he jumped for it and,blinking, hung on for a few
seconds, he was " there". I had no worries after that.
      Thank you for such devotion to duty. I am proud to
know you all.

Sincerely and with
Best Wishes,

Archie Horka, Master,
AMERICAN SCOUT

harbor, an amazing piece of engineering for those days. Because of its length, it was considered a point of great military advantage and a battery stood at its end.   The British ships of war landed troops here in 1768 and later ranged 12 ships in formidable manner about the northeast part of the town.   One of Paul Revere's best known engravings, which can be seen in the historical collection at our State Street Office, depicts this scene and shows Long Wharf as it was in all its impressiveness.   Historically, it is considered Boston's most distinguished wharf. Here, down through the years, vessels of various types and sizes loaded and unloaded their cargoes.   Chartered as "The Proprietors of Boston Pier or the Long Wharf" in 1772, it is one of the earliest American business corporations, and has certainly established a remarkable record for continuous operation.

PILOT #1 AND *ROSEWAY* #2

PRESENT PILOT BOATS

W. Starling Burgess, the famous Massachusetts yacht designer and pioneer airplane builder, son of Edward Burgess, well-known naval architect of his day, designed the *Pilot* which was built for the pilots in 1924 at the J. F. James shipyard at Essex, Mass. She is a spoon-bowed auxiliary schooner equipped with twin-screw diesel engines of 165 horsepower each. Her length is 121 ft. over-all and 98 ft. at the water line, with a 25 ft. beam and she draws 14 ft. 5 in.

The *Roseway,* the latest pilot boat, was built in 1926 also at the James yard. She measures 100 ft. over-all and 94 ft. at the water line, 25 ft. beam and draws 13 ft. Her diesels develop 330 horsepower, the same as those on her sister boat. The *Roseway* was selected as the pilots found, after careful inspection, that she came very near to meeting the specifications of an ideal pilot boat. Built stoutly of oak, she was fit to withstand the heavy seas and boisterous gales which these boats are bound to encounter. She has fully justified the expectations of her owners when they purchased her in 1941 as a replacement for the *Northern Light* which was taken over by the Government for war service.

The *Pilot*

The *Roseway*

THE TWO PILOT BOATS IN SERVICE 1956

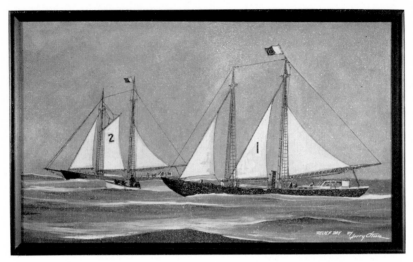

From a painting by Larry O'Toole   *Courtesy of the Pilots of Boston*

RELIEF DAY

Showing an event which occurs each Tuesday when one pilot
boat relieves the other. The boat which is relieved goes to her
home dock at East Boston for checking up and replenishment
of supplies to be ready for her turn the next week or to replace
the other boat in case of emergency. The pilots serve two
weeks on call day and night, followed by one week off.

*   *   *

James Russell Lowell, who has been described as the
"viking of the poets," found great joy in donning a tarpaulin
suit and sailing down through the island passages and far out
into the Bay in one of the swift pilot boats which cruised between the capes of Massachusetts.

In a letter in June of 1859 to his friend Charles Eliot
Norton, famed American scholar, man of letters and professor
of the history of art at Harvard for many years, as well as editor
of "Letters of James Russell Lowell," published by Harper &
Brothers in 1894, Lowell reported that he had been down
Boston harbor on the *Friend* and stated that he enjoyed cruising

in the fine breeze. "Being down the harbor with something
to do and somebody else to do it for you," he wrote, came up
to his notion of real pleasure. He saw the *Friend* put pilots
aboard a bark and a brig before breakfast and thoroughly enjoyed the trip. On leaving the pilot boat Captain James M.
Dolliver presented him with a basket full of lobsters. Lowell
described the Captain as a noble fellow weighing two hundred
and ten pounds — all of which he risked during the previous
winter to save a man from a wrecked ship. He added the query:
"Does it not require more heroism to venture two hundred
weight than a paltry one hundred and forty odd?" The rescue
he mentioned was, of course, that made in February of 1859,
as told in the chapter on Captains Dolliver and Chandler.

*   *   *

"Some like pictures o' women" said Bill,
"An' some likes 'orses best;
But I likes pictures o' ships," said he,
"An' you can keep the rest."

MORE EARLY PILOT BOATS OF BOSTON
are portrayed on the following pages

PILOT BOAT *EDWIN FORREST*

The *Edwin Forrest* built in 1865 was designed by the noted Dennison J. Lawlor to the order of Pilot Captain John Low, whose son of the same name also had a long and distinguished career in piloting. Her wonderful speed was the talk and the toast of the 1870s. She was a consistent winner of races in the 4th of July regattas conducted by the City of Boston.

The painting reproduced above was presented to our Bank by Captain Nathaniel W. Abbott, a former Boston Harbor pilot now retired. It may be seen in the collection at our State Street Office, in the Trust Department.

PILOT BOAT *PET* OF BOSTON

The *Pet*, a boat of 54 tons, steered by means of a tiller, was built in 1866 by Edward E. ("Ned") Costigan at Charlestown, Mass. for Pilot Captain Abel T. Hayden. She was in service for a number of years and was considered a very handsome pilot boat.

The oil painting by Walter F. Lansil reproduced above may be seen in the collection at our State Street Office, in the Trust Department.

Courtesy of Charles M. Wright

PILOT BOAT *SYLPH*

Built at North Weymouth, Mass. in 1878, this 60-ton pilot boat was in the Boston service until she was sold in 1901.

PILOT BOAT *EBEN D. JORDAN*

The oil painting, by the well-known Hendricks A. Hallett of Boston, reproduced above, hangs in the home of Mr. Charles I. Lampee of Winchester, Mass. Mr. Lampee's grandfather, Captain Thomas Cooper, was a friend and admirer of the great merchant of Boston who was one of the founders of the far-famed Jordan Marsh Company. When Captain Cooper had this pilot boat built by Ambrose A. Martin at East Boston in 1883, it was quite natural for him to select the name which she bore for nearly ten years in both the Boston and New York pilot service. Mr. Jordan presented to Captain Cooper a complete set of signal flags for use on his pilot boat namesake. After operating in Boston the *Eben D. Jordan* was sold to pilots of New York. In 1892 she was lost when struck by the S. S. *Saginaw* during a gale off Barnegat, New Jersey.

Courtesy of the Peabody Museum, Salem, Massachusetts

MODEL OF THE PILOT BOAT *LIBERTY*

This model was presented by the Boston pilots to the late Charles H. Taylor when Editor of the Boston "Globe." I. Clarence Bailey, top left, and Frederick L. Bailey, right, both of Kingston, Mass., were included in this illustration because they did a major part of the work in making the model which is now in the collection of the Peabody Museum. The *Liberty* was built at Gloucester, Mass. in 1896 and was in the pilot service until 1934 when she was replaced by the *Northern Light*. She was purchased by the late Roscoe H. Prior, long active in Boston port affairs, and Ephraim W. Higgins of Wellfleet, formerly an officer of the *Leviathan*. She was used as a press boat at the time of President Roosevelt's trip to Campobello in 1936.

From the collection of the Second Bank-State Street Trust Company

The Bark *SACHEM*

Signalling the pilot boat *Hesper* off Minot's Light

The original owner of this water color by C. Myron Clark was aboard the *Hesper* when the *Sachem* was on its way to Boston from the East Indies in 1897. He gave a full description to the artist who painted the picture on special order.

A SECTION OF HEAD OFFICE BANKING ROOMS
111 Franklin Street

STATE STREET OFFICE
Corner State & Congress Streets
Ship models and old prints in an atmosphere reminiscent of
early Colonial counting houses.

SECOND BANK - STATE STREET TRUST COMPANY

UNION TRUST OFFICE
24 Federal Street
Models, prints, etc., depicting the progress of aviation from balloon
and glider days to the present.

STATLER OFFICE
Corner Arlington and Providence Streets

COPLEY SQUARE OFFICE
587 Boylston Street

MASSACHUSETTS AVENUE OFFICE
Corner Mass. Ave. & Boylston St.
At each of our offices we have tried to create an attractive atmosphere for those doing business with us.

SECOND BANK - STATE STREET TRUST COMPANY

Head Office
111 FRANKLIN STREET
BOSTON, MASSACHUSETTS

State Street Office
COR. STATE AND CONGRESS STREETS

Union Trust Office
24 FEDERAL STREET

Statler Office
COR. ARLINGTON AND PROVIDENCE STREETS

Copley Square Office
587 BOYLSTON STREET

Massachusetts Avenue Office
COR. MASS. AVENUE AND BOYLSTON STREET

Sales Finance Department
711 BOYLSTON STREET

★

SAFE DEPOSIT VAULTS AT ALL OFFICES

★

Member
Federal Reserve System
Federal Deposit Insurance Corporation